THE JOY OF IMPERFECTION

A STRESS-FREE GUIDE TO SILENCING YOUR INNER CRITIC, CONQUERING PERFECTIONISM, AND BECOMING THE BEST VERSION OF YOURSELF!

DAMON ZAHARIADES

ARTOFPRODUCTIVITY.COM

OTHER BOOKS BY DAMON ZAHARIADES

∼

The Art Of Saying NO: How To Stand Your Ground, Reclaim Your Time And Energy, And Refuse To Be Taken For Granted (Without Feeling Guilty!)

Are you fed up with people taking you for granted? Learn how to set boundaries, stand your ground, and inspire others' respect in the process!

∼

The Procrastination Cure: 21 Proven Tactics For Conquering Your Inner Procrastinator, Mastering Your Time, And Boosting Your Productivity!

Do you struggle with procrastination? Discover how to take quick action, make fast decisions, and finally overcome your inner procrastinator!

∼

Morning Makeover: How To Boost Your Productivity, Explode Your Energy, and Create An Extraordinary Life - One Morning At A Time!

Would you like to start each day on the right foot? Here's how to create quality morning routines that set you up for more daily success!

~

Fast Focus: A Quick-Start Guide To Mastering Your Attention, Ignoring Distractions, And Getting More Done In Less Time!

Are you constantly distracted? Does your mind wander after just a few minutes? Learn how to develop laser-sharp focus!

~

Small Habits Revolution: 10 Steps To Transforming Your Life Through The Power Of Mini Habits!

Got 5 minutes a day? Use this simple, effective plan for creating any new habit you desire!

~

To-Do List Formula: A Stress-Free Guide To Creating To-Do Lists That Work!

Finally! A step-by-step system for creating to-do lists that'll actually help you to get things done!

~

The 30-Day Productivity Plan: Break The 30 Bad Habits That Are Sabotaging Your Time Management - One Day At A Time!

Need a daily action plan to boost your productivity? This 30-day guide is the solution to your time management woes!

~

Digital Detox: Unplug To Reclaim Your Life

Addicted to technology? Here's how to disconnect and enjoy real, meaningful connections that lead to long-term happiness.

~

The Time Chunking Method: A 10-Step Action Plan For Increasing Your Productivity

It's one of the most popular time management strategies used today. Double your productivity with this easy 10-step system.

~

For a complete list, please visit

http://artofproductivity.com/my-books/

YOUR FREE GIFT

~

As my way of saying thanks for your purchase, I'd like to offer you my 40-page action guide titled *Catapult Your Productivity! The Top 10 Habits You Must Develop To Get More Things Done.*

It's in PDF format, so you can easily print it out and read it at your leisure. This guide will show you how to develop core habits that'll help you to get more done in less time.

You can get immediate access to *Catapult Your Productivity* by clicking the link below and joining my mailing list:

http://artofproductivity.com/free-gift/

NOTABLE QUOTABLES ABOUT PERFECTION

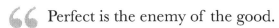

❝ Perfect is the enemy of the good.
    - Voltaire

❝ Perfectionism is the voice of the oppressor.
    - Anne Lamott

❝ Perfectionism is just fear in really good shoes.
    - Elizabeth Gilbert

PERFECTIONISM: A RECIPE FOR CHRONIC UNHAPPINESS

~

Many of us grew up with the idea that perfectionism is a worthy goal. Many of the people in our lives reinforce that notion. Our parents, teachers, coaches, and bosses encourage perfectionistic behavior, expressing dissatisfaction over flawed results, regardless of how minor the flaws.

Being *imperfect* is often seen as a weakness. It's considered a personal and professional defect.

But is this perception true? Is imperfection really a shortcoming?

I'm going to make the opposite case in this book. I'm going to highlight the many consequences of perfectionistic behavior, and in the process show you there's great joy in *imperfection*. I'll then give you a strategic guide that'll help you to make the transition and embrace the latter.

Don't be fooled by those who encourage perfectionism. Don't doubt your worth because your efforts fail to meet their approval. It takes great courage to set aside rigid, self-defeating behavior and pursue authenticity.

All of us are flawed. All of us make mistakes. Perfection is an illusion, and the struggle to achieve it can only lead to disappointment, frustration, and self-criticism.

I suspect there's a perfectionist in each of us. For some, it hides in the shadows, whispering of incompetence and subtly fueling doubt and shame. In others, it takes a more active role. It impels them to strive for faultlessness in everything they do, producing unnecessary stress and anxiety in the process.

In *The Joy Of Imperfection*, we're going to turn this mindset on its head. I'm going to show you how to quiet your inner perfectionist. You'll get a step-by-step blueprint for not only abandoning the obsessive, useless pursuit of perfection, but being 100% confident in your authentic, imperfect nature.

In the next section, I'll describe how perfectionism negatively impacted my life. Don't be surprised if you notice hints of your own life in my story.

MY NAME IS DAMON, AND I'M A
RECOVERING PERFECTIONIST

~

I t's 1980.
I'm competing in a swimming event. At ten years old, I'm already familiar with the custom. I've been training and competing since the age of six. My family is hopeful that I'll qualify to compete in the 1988 Olympics.

I come in third place, and feel dejected. What some might consider a success is, to me, a pitiful failure. I'm too young to think of success and failure as a binary equation. But I do nonetheless.

Five years later, after continuously failing to take the top spot in my events, I'm demoralized and miserable. There's no joy left in the sport for me, and I eventually give it up.

It's 1985.

I'm fifteen years old, practicing guitar in my bedroom. I'm playing scales over and over, cringing each time I miss a note. I'm playing chords, berating myself each time they sound muddy, or the chord changes are less than pristine.

In my mind, there are only two possible outcomes: perfect or imperfect. Flawless or flawed. There's nothing in between, and the latter state is unacceptable. Unsurprisingly, each practice session ends in discouragement and frustration. I eventually give up playing the guitar altogether.

It's 1995.

I work for one of the largest money management companies in the world. I take pride in my abilities, and go to great lengths to make sure my handiwork is without errors.

The problem is, perfection is difficult to sustain when tight deadlines loom. I put in extra time to compensate. But burning the candle at both ends is a recipe for burnout. The quality of my work declines; mistakes creep in and go unnoticed by my fatigued eyes. I'm too tired to appreciate the irony - my obsession with perfection is draining my energy and eroding my attention and causing me to make errors. I eventually quit my well-paying job in aggravation.

Perfectionism was a frequent stumbling block for me beginning in childhood. It negatively affected every area of my life, from my studies to my relationships. Worse, each time I failed to live up to my unreasonably high standards, I castigated myself and grew more miserable.

I finally figured out how to overcome this Achilles heel. It wasn't easy, but it was definitely worth the time and effort. Embracing imperfection had an immediate, positive effect on my stress levels, confidence, and sense of self-worth. In short, it improved my quality of life.

In the following pages, I'll show you exactly what I did to curb my perfectionistic tendencies. If you have difficulty accepting anything less than perfect from yourself, and would like to change that pattern, you're in the right place.

Let's start by taking a look at the two main types of perfectionism. Note whether you recognize aspects of them in yourself.

ADAPTIVE VS. MALADAPTIVE
PERFECTIONISM

~

There are many flavors of perfectionism. But each of them has roots in one of two main types: *adaptive* or *maladaptive*.

Adaptive Perfectionism

This category of perfectionism is defined as endeavoring to meet high standards, but recognizing that true perfection is an unreasonable expectation. Adaptive perfectionists are driven by the satisfaction they experience when they apply extreme effort toward accomplishing their goals.

An example is a student who studies all night, sacrificing food and sleep, to score high on a final exam scheduled for the following day. This student realizes it's unlikely he'll get a perfect score. But for him, the intense effort he devotes to studying is its own reward.

Some experts consider adaptive perfectionism to be a healthy form of perfectionism. They note that it aids people in accomplishing their goals.

Others, such as Paul Hewitt, Ph.D, co-author of the oft-cited Multidimensional Perfectionism Scale, feel differently. Hewitt has opined *"I don't think needing to be perfect is in any way adaptive."*

It's neither my intent nor my desire to weigh in on this particular matter. Rather, to advance the aim of this book, I believe it's useful to simply contrast *adaptive* perfectionism with *maladaptive* perfectionism.

Maladaptive Perfectionism

This category of perfectionism is defined as striving to meet unrealistic goals, and expecting to accomplish them every time. Maladaptive perfectionists aggressively maintain unreasonably high standards, and are highly critical of themselves when they fail to meet them.

An example is a student who studies all night to achieve a perfect score on a final exam, and considers a lesser score to be a personal failure. This perceived failure leads to self-recrimination, higher stress levels, lower self-esteem, and depression.

The maladaptive perfectionist mistakenly believes he can exert full control over his environment. Ergo, he believes himself to be entirely at fault for unfavorable outcomes.

This type of perfectionism is universally considered unhealthy. All experts agree on this point.

Subtypes Of Perfectionism

I noted above that perfectionism comes in many flavors, though most - if not all - of them can be categorized as adaptive or maladaptive. This categorization is paramount to our purpose in *The Joy Of Imperfection*: reversing maladaptive perfectionism.

Having said that, it's useful to be familiar with these various subtypes, if only to recognize their respective nuances in our lives. To that end, let's quickly define the most common varieties (you'll notice a bit of overlap between them).

- **Self-oriented perfectionism**: imposing exceedingly high standards on oneself.
- **Socially prescribed perfectionism**: believing that others expect perfection from oneself.
- **Other-oriented perfectionism**: expecting others to be perfect.
- **Neurotic perfectionism**: striving for perfection, spurred by the belief that being perfect will result in others' approval.

- **Principled perfectionism**: struggling to achieve one's perception of moral flawlessness.
- **Hyper-attentive perfectionism**: focusing on the object of one's attention to the point that every detail must be closely scrutinized.
- **Narcissistic perfectionism**: showing off abilities or knowledge to reinforce others' perception of one's ideal self.
- **Emotional perfectionism**: believing one should be in complete control over one's emotions.

Again, we're going to focus primarily on maladaptive perfectionism throughout *The Joy Of Imperfection*. It's not important to memorize the various subtypes listed above. Rather, recall that some experts consider *all* types of perfectionism to be maladaptive, and worth reversing.

In the next section, we'll explore the typical mindset of a perfectionist. Don't be surprised if some of the traits we're about to cover strike a personal chord.

THE MINDSET OF THE PERFECTIONIST
(WHY WE PURSUE PERFECTION)

~

I f you're a true perfectionist, the idea of being flawless eats away at you. It dominates your mind space. Everything you do immediately undergoes a rigid self-critique. This critique sets the stage for self-criticism whenever you fail to meet your impractically high, self-imposed standards.

But why does this happen in the first place? Why are perfectionists driven to achieve perfection?

It turns out, there are many potential reasons. All of them stem from fear, anxiety, unhappiness, and/or an unfair conviction regarding how one's worth should be measured.

For example, many perfectionists fear failure. They see everything in black and white, and view the results of their actions through that inflexible lens. They either succeed or fail. There's no middle ground.

The possibility of failure makes perfectionists miserable. They attempt to squash this fear by striving harder to be flawless. Unfortunately, because perfection is a mirage, this is ultimately self-defeating behavior.

Another trigger is shame. Many perfectionists feel inadequate in one or more ways. They believe they're not athletic enough, pretty enough, smart enough, rich enough, motivated enough, or dedicated enough.

In short, they feel they're not *good* enough. Whether this perception is true doesn't matter. They *believe* it.

Perfectionists pursue flawlessness to counter this feeling. They tell themselves, *"If I do everything perfectly, I'll prove that I'm good enough."* This mindset is a precarious one because no one can successfully maintain this ridiculous standard over the long run.

Many perfectionists feel they need to be flawless so their friends, family members, coworkers, and even strangers will think highly of them. They're overly concerned with how they're perceived by others. They assume people will think less of them if they make a mistake. So they take great pains to ensure that doesn't happen.

The effort inevitably leads to frustration and despair. After all, mistakes are unavoidable. They're a part of being human.

Another trigger is a sense of chaos. Many perfectionists feel disorganized to the point that they believe their lives are out of their control. Their offices are messy. Their homes are untidy. Their vehicles look as if they've been living in them for weeks.

These individuals strive to be perfect to bring order to their seemingly chaotic world. Getting organized isn't enough for them. Instead, they attempt to make every personal space flawless. In their minds, their offices must be immaculate. Their homes must be spotless. Their vehicles must appear pristine and unblemished - inside and out.

Of course, nothing remains immaculate, spotless, or pristine over the long run. Such expectations are unrealistic. Unfortunately, the perfectionist refuses to acknowledge this fact, and drives him or herself crazy trying to achieve the unattainable.

Reversing The Perfectionist Mindset

All perfectionists see things in black and white. Succeed versus fail. Good versus bad. Acceptable versus unacceptable.

There's no room for error.

If you struggle with this self-defeating mindset, and desperately want to change, I have good news for you. *The Joy Of Imperfection* will show you how to reverse this way of thinking.

It won't happen overnight. But if you put into practice the ideas and tactics found in the following pages, you will eventually overcome this debilitating habit.

WHAT YOU'LL LEARN IN THE JOY OF IMPERFECTION

~

The Joy Of Imperfection will help you to curb your perfectionistic behavior. If you're the type of person for whom flawlessness is a compulsion, this book will help you to regain control of that impulse.

There are plenty of books that address the psychology of perfectionism. They discuss perfectionism in the context of cognitive and behavioral research.

We're not going to do that here. The Joy Of Imperfection is an action guide. It has a practical purpose: to help you conquer perfectionism in your life.

In the event you're interested in the psychology behind the habit, I've included a number of links at the end of this section. They'll take you to scientific studies that address the cognitive aspects of perfectionism. (Note that some require a fee for access.)

The Joy Of Imperfection is organized into three parts. Following is a quick breakdown of what you'll find in each of them.

Part I

Reversing any bad habit or unhealthy behavior requires identifying an impetus, or reason for doing so. This reason will give you the motivation to continue when your brain resists. To this end, it's important to be aware of the many ways perfectionistic behavior negatively impacts your life.

In Part I, we'll talk about the downsides of perfectionism. Some of them are less than obvious, and you may be surprised to discover which ones are affecting you.

Part II

It's one thing to strive for excellence. That's a worthy goal shared by high achievers from all walks of life. It's another thing entirely to obsess about being flawless. This rigid perspective about your performance unavoidably leads to frustration, anxiety, and even depression.

In Part II, we'll examine signals that indicate your perfectionism is out of control. If you're a lifelong perfectionist, you may be unaware of the extent to which the habit governs your thought process and actions. Here, you'll learn to recognize the warning signs.

Part III

This part of *The Joy Of Imperfection* provides a strategic action plan for overcoming your perfectionistic tendencies. If you've tried to vanquish this mindset in the past, you know it's not as easy as deciding to "let things go." A more methodical approach is necessary for success.

In Part III, I'll take you through a step-by-step program that'll chip away at your perfectionistic proclivities. By the time you complete the program, you'll be able to successfully curb this self-defeating psychology.

BECAUSE YOU'RE READING this book, it's safe to assume you struggle with perfectionism. Moreover, you recognize that it's negatively affecting your life. The good news is, you've taken an important step toward finally gaining control over this compulsion.

We have a lot to cover in the following pages. But I promise we'll move quickly so you can take advantage of the advice as soon as possible.

Studies On Perfectionism

Following are several studies that address the cognitive aspects of perfectionism. I love this type of stuff, so I found them interesting. But fair warning: a couple of them are quite dense.

Hill, Andrew P., Witcher, Chad S.G., Gotwals, John K., & Leyland, Anne F. (2015) A Qualitative Study of Perfectionism Among Self-Identified Perfectionists in Sport and the Performing Arts (https://www.apa.org/pubs/journals/features/spy-spy0000041.pdf)

Hill, Andrew P., Curran, Thomas (2015) Multidimensional Perfectionism and Burnout: A Meta-Analysis (http://journals.sagepub.com/doi/abs/10.1177/1088868 315596286)

Kilbert, J.J., Langhinrichsen-Rohling, J., & Saito, M. (2005). Adaptive and maladaptive aspects of self-oriented versus socially prescribed perfectionism. (https://muse.jhu.edu/article/180085)

Schuler, Patricia A. (1999) Perfectionistic Gifted Adolescents in a Rural Middle School (http://files.eric.ed.gov/fulltext/ED430352.pdf)

Frost, Randy O., Marten, Patricia, Lahart, Cathleen, & Rosenblate, Robin (1990) The dimensions of perfectionism (https://link.springer.com/article/10.1007%2FBF0117296 7)

Hewitt, Paul L., & Flett, Gordon L. (1990). Perfectionism and depression: A multidimensional analysis. (http://psycnet.apa.org/record/1991-04621-001)

HOW TO GET MAXIMUM VALUE FROM THIS BOOK

∽

You've likely read personal development books in the past. So you know from experience that the books themselves aren't the key to success. Rather, it's what you do with the information contained in them.

The Joy Of Imperfection is no different in that regard. It offers plenty of actionable advice that can literally change your life. But if you don't apply the advice, it'll go to waste.

To that end, I've included numerous exercises in *Part III: A Complete Action Plan For Overcoming Perfectionism.* I strongly encourage you to do them.

If you're like me, you'll be tempted to skip the exercises and continue reading. I urge you to resist that temptation. You'll gain so much more value from the action plan if you spend a couple moments doing the exercises at the end of the sections.

If you prefer to read *The Joy Of Imperfection* in its entirety, and then go back to do the exercises afterward, that's fine. It's less than ideal, but you'll still benefit from them. Moreover, the material in the book is organized so you can quickly and easily find specific sections at your leisure. That allows you to tailor the action plan to your needs.

Also, you've no doubt noticed *The Joy Of Imperfection* is a short book. That's by design. In my experience, the most effective way to reverse any self-defeating behavior is through the application of healthy, countervailing practices - hence, the exercises in *Part III*. You don't need a 400-page opus that dives deeply into psychology and neuroscience. It would only slow you down.

In my opinion, shorter is better. This way, you can glean the information you *need*, and get down to the business of effecting positive change in your life.

I encourage you to read thoughtfully and engage with the material. Mull over the various aspects of perfectionism covered in each section. Do the exercises.

By the time you finish reading *The Joy Of Imperfection*, you'll have everything you need to leave your perfectionistic tendencies behind you forever.

PART I

12 WAYS PERFECTIONISM NEGATIVELY IMPACTS YOUR LIFE

∿

The pursuit of flawlessness is rooted in a desire for acceptance. Many perfectionists crave validation from others, such as their friends, family members, coworkers, and bosses. Doing a perfect job results in praise and accolades, which perfectionists use to measure their self-worth.

Other perfectionists desire *personal* validation. For them, doing a perfect job serves as self-reinforcement. It reassures them of their value.

Still others seek both. They yearn for validation from others as well as themselves, and go to great lengths to obtain it.

There's a dark side to this inclination. When you

constantly strive to be perfect, you train your brain to accept nothing less. Consequently, your brain avoids taking any action that might lead to mistakes. In many cases, this means avoiding taking any action at all (i.e. procrastination).

In *Part I*, we're going to take a close look at the many ways in which your perfectionism is affecting your life.

#1 - IT MAKES YOU LESS ADAPTIVE TO CHANGING CIRCUMSTANCES

∿

The world is complex and fast-paced, and becomes increasingly so with each passing year. Circumstances change more quickly than ever, often leaving us with only two options: adapt or be left behind.

Adapting to change isn't easy, even when the changes are positive. Change introduces uncertainty and risk. So most of us resist it.

Perfectionists are even more resistant to change. It wrests control from their hands. It makes them feel as if they have less influence over their environment. This feeling, in turn, elevates their sense of vulnerability because they presume the odds that something will go wrong are greater.

Perfectionists find this situation unacceptable.

The problem is, changing circumstances are an ever-present variable in our lives. We constantly experience change at home, at our jobs, and at school. We face it in the relationships we share with our friends and family members. We encounter it in everything we do, from shopping and dining out to exercising and cleaning our homes.

The healthy response to any type of imposed change is adaptation. We accept the change, analyze it, and determine how best to adapt to it. Then, we move on with our lives.

This is a major challenge for the perfectionist. He or she dreads new situations, and takes pains to avoid them. Unfortunately, because change is inevitable, avoidance is a losing proposition.

Worse, it's one that ultimately leads to mental, emotional, and in some cases even physical stress. The loss of control borne of changing circumstances doesn't preclude the perfectionist from blaming himself or herself when things go wrong. He or she still internalizes the situation as a personal failure. This perceived failure is then used by the perfectionist to measure the worth of his or her performance.

It's decidedly unfair. Unfortunately, this fact doesn't prevent the perfectionist from feeling discouraged, frustrated, and demoralized. These negative feelings, if left unchecked, can grow to the point that they become overwhelming. This, in turn, will make it even more difficult for the perfectionist to meet his or her impossibly high standards going forward. The result is a vicious cycle of perceived failures followed by self-recrimination.

#2 - IT ENCOURAGES AN ALL-OR-NOTHING MENTALITY

∼

66 *If I can't do it perfectly, I may as well not do it at all."*

MANY PERFECTIONISTS HAVE THIS ATTITUDE. They have a task or project in mind. They know their desired result. And they know what's required to achieve it. The problem is, they doubt their ability to take action without making mistakes.

This isn't a problem for *non*-perfectionists. Non-perfectionists recognize that mistakes are par for the course. They realize the important thing is to make progress toward their goals. They value *incremental* progress more than perfect progress.

Not so for perfectionists. Perfectionists loathe the possibility that they might make mistakes. This potential outcome paralyzes them, hampering their productivity and performance in two ways.

First, they're disinclined to take action. Facing a task or project for which they feel unready, they shut down. They refuse to start, fearing their actions will inevitably lead to criticism - from others as well as themselves. This unhealthy response prevents the perfectionist from completing tasks and pursuing personal interests.

For example, let's suppose you want to write a best-selling novel. But you realize there are obstacles, many of which are likely to cause you to stumble. Rather than pushing forward, addressing these obstacles as you encounter them, you decide against starting your novel.

If you can't do it perfectly, you'd rather not do it at all.

The second way an all-or-nothing outlook hurts perfectionists is that it makes them more inclined to quit when unanticipated problems arise. Recall from the previous section that perfectionists have difficulty adapting to changing circumstances. They feel out of control. Worse, they internalize negative outcomes, even when they're not to blame. The result? They're prepared and predisposed to give up when things go awry.

For example, suppose you've decided to pay off your credit card debt. You devise a plan whereby you'll pay an extra $1,000 a month until you reduce your debt to $0. Things go as planned for a few months. But then, unexpectedly, your vehicle breaks down, requiring costly repairs.

This unanticipated problem disrupts your plan. The following month, rather than resuming your intention to pay off your credit card balances, you give up. In fact, you go shopping to counteract the intense feeling of discouragement.

An all-or-nothing attitude can be debilitating. It can stop you from doing what you want to do, and prevent you from accomplishing your goals. Whether that involves paying off your credit cards, decluttering your home, or starting a new weight loss program, it can mentally paralyze you.

But don't worry. I'll show you how to overcome this tendency later in this book.

#3 - IT DISCOURAGES YOU FROM TAKING RISKS

❦

We have to venture outside our comfort zones if we want to achieve personal growth. The problem is, doing so imposes a degree of risk. With risk, outcomes become less certain, and the odds of failure - or at least *perceived* failure - increase.

This is a distressing situation for perfectionists. For them, failure is detestable. The mere possibility irks them.

This attitude toward failure is entrenched in their brains. Although we tend to think of perfectionism as the pursuit of flawlessness, it's actually spurred by fear of failure.

For this reason, perfectionists gravitate toward circumstances that guarantee success. Such situations allow them to predict outcomes with reasonable accuracy, giving them a sense of comfort and confidence.

Risk spoils this objective. Uncertainty chips away at the perfectionist's self-assurance, leaving him or her frustrated, discouraged, and paralyzed with indecision.

It's important to recognize that life is about taking risks. We embrace risk - consciously or otherwise - when we meet new people, pursue personal interests and professional opportunities, and invest for the future.

We take a risk when we get married. We take a risk when we leave one job for another. We take risks when we start businesses, cook new meals, and visit unfamiliar vacation destinations.

In short, risk is a prerequisite for fully enjoying life's rich abundance.

In this light, perfectionistic behavior negatively affects our quality of life. It prevents us from pursuing anything that jeopardizes our sense of control, including activities that would otherwise prove deeply rewarding.

This predicament isn't permanent. You can radically change your outlook with the right action plan. (We'll get to that in *Part III.*)

#4 - IT ALLOWS NEGATIVE SELF-TALK TO GAIN A FOOTHOLD

~

At first, it seems counterintuitive that perfectionism is associated with a low self-image. After all, perfectionists take pride in their flawlessness. Their satisfaction at having done something perfectly would seem to preclude self-image issues.

But it makes sense when you consider that those who hold themselves to unreasonably high standards beat themselves up whenever they fail to meet them. It's a familiar pattern: strive for perfection, make mistakes, feel discouraged.

This is followed by self-recrimination. The perfectionist tells himself or herself:

- *"That was a stupid mistake."*

- *"You should have been better prepared."*
- *"[Tom or Elaine] would have done a much better job."*
- *"People aren't going to like you."*
- *"You failed again."*

This negative self-talk is hurtful. It reinforces the misguided notion that the perfectionist must always be flawless. It whispers of incompetence and lack of ability when things go wrong. Worse, it informs the perfectionist's belief system regarding what is acceptable and what is not. These beliefs, faulty at their core, inevitably stoke feelings of shame and guilt.

The perfectionist, pummeled repeatedly by this negative self-talk, eventually becomes fearful of taking action. His or her belief system maintains that anything short of perfection is unacceptable. So the perfectionist refuses to act, fearing that he or she will fail to measure up.

This paralysis can take a heavy toll on every area of the perfectionist's life. His or her performance at work may suffer. His or her relationships may suffer. And perceived weaknesses might trigger a pervasive, debilitating sense of inadequacy.

The negative self-talk eventually batters the perfectionist's confidence to the point that it makes him or her feel worthless. Once this self-destructive attitude takes root, it becomes difficult to remove. Worse, the constant self-criticism is toxic. It prevents the individual from pursuing personal and professional growth, celebrating personal achievements, and sensibly measuring his or her worth.

The words we say to ourselves are just as powerful as the words we say to others. When we silently berate ourselves for failing to meet impossibly high standards, we do significant damage to our emotional health.

Here's the good news: once you let go of your perfectionistic tendencies, your inner critic will hold far less power and influence over you.

#5 - IT IMPAIRS YOUR ABILITY TO MAKE DECISIONS

~

Perfectionists struggle with indecisiveness. Uncertainty about the future threatens their sense of stability. Forced to choose between uncertain outcomes, they're tormented by anxiety and indecision.

They'd rather make *no* decision than make a wrong one.

This mental paralysis stems from the all-or-nothing attitude we discussed earlier. People with perfectionistic tendencies see things in black and white. Their performance is either perfect or flawed. Results are either good or bad. Outcomes are determined to be successes or failures.

It's no wonder perfectionists have difficulty making decisions. Because they hold themselves to such rigid standards, uncertainty about the future gives rise to significant stress.

It's not just the big, important decisions that paralyze perfectionists. Small, inconsequential decisions can be just as difficult for them.

For example, they agonize over choosing the "perfect" driving route to their destination. They brood over choosing the "perfect" restaurant at which to meet their friends. They worry about choosing the "perfect" outfit to wear to work.

None of these decisions are life-changing. Choosing the wrong driving route may cause a small delay, but nothing more. Choosing the wrong restaurant won't matter among friends. The wrong outfit is likely to go unnoticed by coworkers.

Yet small decisions such as these are a constant source of stress for perfectionists. They may be less terrifying than bigger decisions - e.g. whether to sell one's house or whether to change one's career - but they still cause cognitive logjams and mental paralysis.

Perfectionists wrongly believe that refusing to choose between options with uncertain outcomes is the path that imposes the least risk. In truth, indecision is *worse* than making a wrong decision. It prevents you from moving forward. It causes you to become stuck in the present via perpetual delay.

Indecision also prevents you from learning from your mistakes. Such lessons are a crucial factor in experiencing personal and professional development.

The ability to make quick and definitive decisions is empowering. It tells your brain that you're able to take calculated risks. It also tells your brain that uncertainty is nothing to fear. Worst-case scenarios rarely come to pass, and on the rare occasions they do, they're seldom as grave as we imagine them to be.

#6 - IT MAKES YOU PRONE TO PROCRASTINATION

~

Procrastination is a common side effect of perfectionism. It stems from two factors.

First, it's linked to indecisiveness, which we discussed in the previous section. The inability to choose between competing options, all of which impose a degree of uncertainty, induces the perfectionist to delay taking action. The threat of failure causes him or her mental paralysis.

Second, perfectionistic individuals procrastinate when they're faced with tasks and projects that seem too daunting. Because of their all-or-nothing mentality, any endeavor is a succeed-or-fail proposition. If they suspect they'll be unable to perform to perfection, or doing so will require too much time or effort, they're likely to postpone taking action.

Whichever of the two triggers is present, one thing is certain: a person whose happiness is contingent upon effecting predictably perfect outcomes will be apprehensive when failure is a possibility. He or she will be racked with anxiety regarding what to do. Over time, this anxiety reinforces the notion that postponing action is a good idea.

Unfortunately, procrastination imposes its own set of consequences. It hampers productivity. It leads to missed opportunities. It erodes self-esteem. In severe cases, it can destroy careers and ruin relationships.

The good news is that curbing your perfectionistic tendencies can help resolve your procrastination problem. Once you give yourself permission to be less than perfect, you'll become more willing to be wrong and make mistakes. You'll see such circumstances as learning opportunities rather than personal failures.

This is a much healthier attitude. It'll gradually erode your fear of uncertain outcomes, making you less inclined to delay taking action. It'll also whittle down your all-or-nothing mindset, revealing that your endeavors are critical for growth rather than just part of a misguided succeed-or-fail dichotomy.

#7 - IT INCREASES YOUR STRESS LEVELS

~

Perfectionistic behavior places you under constant pressure. You perpetually feel that your performance is under scrutiny. Everything you do is being judged by everyone around you. When others aren't available to judge your performance, your inner critic picks up the slack.

It's no wonder studies find that perfectionistic behavior is associated with stress, anxiety, and depression.[1] At least one study has even linked perfectionism to suicidal thoughts.[2]

What's behind the nonstop stress? For most perfectionists, it's an inner voice that relentlessly drives them to be flawless. No other outcome will suffice.

It's one thing for this voice to spring to life when stakes

are high. For example, a heart surgeon can't afford to make mistakes while performing an operation. Flawlessness is an expectation, at least in the context of the surgeon's job. (Incidentally, this is the reason many surgeons suffer from high stress levels and burnout.[3])

It's another thing entirely for one's inner voice to come alive when the stakes are low. For example, suppose the aforementioned surgeon maintained his or her perfection-istic standards at home. He or she tackles every task, from cooking meals to choosing clothes for the following day, with the same draconian obsessiveness.

In such a scenario, the surgeon's stress would fail to dissipate after he or she leaves the hospital. Instead, it would become an ever-present ornament to his or her lifestyle.

Chronic stress is no stranger to perfectionists. You probably know this from experience. Unfortunately, if it's left unchecked, chronic stress can impose severe conse-quences on your body and mind.

Persistently high stress can affect every part in your body, from your cardiovascular and respiratory systems to your musculoskeletal, gastrointestinal, and endocrine systems. It can also cause insomnia, grumpiness, and depression, and hamper your ability to focus. Research shows that chronic stress can even alter the structure of your brain.[4]

Again, here's the good news: curbing your inner perfec-tionist will lower your stress levels. That's what we'll focus on in *Part III: A Complete Action Plan For Overcoming Perfectionism.*

[1]
http://www.apa.org/monitor/may06/perfectionists.aspx

[2]
http://onlinelibrary.wiley.com/doi/10.1111/jopy.12333/abstract

[3]
https://jamanetwork.com/journals/jamasurgery/fullarticle/404847

[4]
http://www.nature.com/mp/journal/v19/n12/full/mp2013190a.html

#8 - IT HAMPERS YOUR CREATIVITY

~

Risk is inherent in any type of creative process. It manifests in the form of external feedback. An individual's "product" - the end result of his or her efforts - invites both praise and criticism.

This scenario is intolerable to the perfectionist. Highly averse to risk and uncertainty, he or she is inclined to follow processes that have led to success in the past. This means doing such things in the same manner, over and over, with no deviation.

Perfectionism and creativity mix like oil and vinegar. They cannot occupy the same space.

Perfectionists fear the unpredictable. Creatives embrace it. Perfectionists crave acclaim, and go to great lengths to guarantee they receive it - from others and themselves. Creatives recognize that acclaim is merely one of many possible outcomes. They realize their efforts may also attract disapproval and recrimination. Perfectionists loathe uncertainty while creatives face uncertainty with aplomb. (I'm painting with a broad brush. There are certainly creatives who crumble under criticism.)

Novelist Anne Lamott, in her book *Bird By Bird*, noted that *"perfectionism will ruin your writing, blocking inventiveness and playfulness."* She was speaking to authors about the value of being willing to make mistakes. But in my opinion, her quote can be applied universally. Perfectionistic behavior will always impede creativity. The perfectionist's fear of failure - or at least, what he or she *perceives* as failure - all but guarantees it.

I relate to this on a personal level. When I used to sit down to write, I'd be petrified. My inner perfectionist would whisper that nothing short of perfection would suffice. So I would agonize over every word. I'd edit myself viciously, writing passages and deleting them seconds later. Expressing my thoughts in creative ways became an insurmountable challenge. My proclivity for perfection cramped my creativity.

In short, I couldn't write.

It was only after I figured out how to silence my inner critic that I was able to write with confidence. And it had a massive impact on my writing productivity. Moreover, silencing my inner critic did more than just improve my creativity. It also allowed me to find joy in the process of creating something in the absence of fear.

I'm willing to bet you'll have the same experience. The moment you give yourself permission to make mistakes, your perfectionism will no longer have a stranglehold on your creativity.

#9 - IT MAKES YOU UNPREPARED FOR UNANTICIPATED PROBLEMS

~

One of the most valuable skills we learn throughout our lives is the ability to solve problems. This skill is crucial to our careers, relationships, and personal pursuits. We use it daily, unraveling challenges, dealing with setbacks, and making decisions when our path forward is either obstructed or uncertain.

The ability to do this is critical to success in every area of our lives. Our problem-solving skills allow us to confront hurdles head-on and figure out ways to move forward.

This is a major stumbling block for anyone who strives for flawlessness. Perfectionistic individuals become frustrated whenever something fails to go according to plan. Because they judge themselves harshly when their actions fail to produce perfect results, this ultimately leads to self-criticism.

Earlier, we noted that perfectionists have difficulty adapting to changing circumstances. Such changes erode their confidence because they feel unable to influence their environment.

This lack of control causes the perfectionist to shut down. He or she would rather delay action until conditions are perfect rather than forge ahead. If delaying action isn't possible, the perfectionist will act, but become highly critical of his or her work. The fact that an unanticipated problem arose will not alleviate his or her guilt or feelings of inadequacy and shame.

For example, suppose you're planning to give a Powerpoint presentation to your coworkers. The moment you start your presentation, you discover that your laptop (on which your Powerpoint slides reside) has stopped working.

What should you do in this scenario?

If you're a diehard perfectionist, your first thought will be to postpone the presentation. However, because your coworkers arranged their schedules to attend, and may not be available at a later date, let's assume postponing it isn't an option. You must move forward, using your memory to reconstruct the content.

Regardless of how effectively you present the material, and how many kudos you receive from those in attendance, you're going to beat yourself up. Why? Because things didn't go perfectly according to plan, and you perceive any outcome that's imperfect to be a personal failure.

This perspective is what prevents the perfectionist from facing problems head-on, brainstorming creative solutions, and deciding between flawed options. It prevents him or her from developing an effective problem-solving framework, and using it to achieve success despite unanticipated obstacles.

By the time you've finished reading *The Joy Of Imperfection*, you'll be well on your way to correcting these issues.

#10 - IT CAN LEAD TO FRUSTRATION, ANXIETY, AND DEPRESSION

∾

L et's stop for a moment and ponder the negative effects of perfectionism we've covered thus far.

Perfectionism impairs our ability to adapt to changing circumstances and new situations. It discourages us from taking risks, and thereby hampers our personal growth. It encourages negative self-talk, and fuels self-criticism. It inhibits our ability to make decisions. It obstructs our creativity. And it prevents us from solving unexpected problems.

Is it any wonder that a life spent in pursuit of flawlessness inevitably leads to frustration?

Unfortunately, the symptoms of a perfectionistic life extend much further. They can include panic attacks, depression, and even suicidal thoughts.

A study published in the journal *PLoS One* in 2012 examined the connection between perfectionism and anxiety disorders among intellectually gifted children.[1] The authors found that such children, at least the ones studied, presented with a higher anxiety level.

A paper written in 2004 by psychologists Gordon Flett and Paul Hewitt for the *Journal of Rational-Emotive & Cognitive-Behavior Therapy* explored the link between perfectionism and anxiety and depression. The authors pointed to past research showing empirical evidence that perfectionism was associated with higher levels of both traits. [2]

A 2006 report on suicides in Alaska noted that 56% of those who committed suicide between September 2003 and August 2006 were described as perfectionists by others.[3]

The relationship between perfectionism and anxiety, depression, and suicide is a complicated one. Many experts claim the ceaseless pursuit of flawlessness is an obsessive-compulsive disorder (OCD). To that end, they believe it's a natural trigger for panic attacks, social phobia, and depression.

If you're experiencing anxiety, and it's related to your perfectionistic behavior, keep reading. You'll find that once you give yourself permission to be imperfect and make mistakes, your anxiety will melt away.

[1] Guignard, Jacques-Henri, Jacquet, Anne-Yvonee, & Lubart, Todd (2012) Perfectionism and Anxiety: A Paradox

in Intellectual Giftedness?
(https://www.ncbi.nlm.nih.gov/pmc/articles/PMC34084
83/

[2] Flett, Gordon L. & Hewitt, Paul L. (2004) The Cognitive and Treatment Aspects Of Perfectionism

[3] Alaska State-wide Suicide Prevention Council (2006)
Alaska Suicide Follow-back Study: Final Report
(http://dhss.alaska.gov/SuicidePrevention/Documents/pd
fs_sspc/sspcfollowback2-07.pdf)

#11 - IT CAN HARM YOUR RELATIONSHIPS

~

Perfectionists are intolerant of mistakes, in themselves *and others*. They hold the people around them to the same high standards they impose upon themselves.

When things go according to plan, perfectionists are happy and relieved. When things go "off script," they become stressed, angry, and fearful. Their inflexible, easily aggravated stance can make their friends, family members, and coworkers miserable.

Part of the problem is that perfectionists often struggle with low self-esteem. This state is born of guilt and shame, which are triggered by ongoing self-flagellation over perceived failures. Perfectionists' low evaluation of their intrinsic worth causes them to withdraw from those who care about them. If this situation is left unresolved, it can take a severe toll on their relationships.

Another part of the problem is that perfectionists measure others' efforts according to whether the results meet impossible expectations. They set their friends, family members, and coworkers up for failure, becoming judgmental when their unrealistic standards aren't met.

Such rigidness is unpleasant. Over time, it becomes intolerable.

Here's a personal example…

While attending college, I played guitar in a garage band. Because I was a staunch perfectionist, every note had to be perfect. That alone was bad enough. But I held the drummer and vocalist to the same unreasonable benchmark. If the drummer was off by a microsecond, or the vocalist hit an off-key note, I'd stop everything and point out their mistakes.

I was hard to be around. And it hurt my relationships with my drummer and vocalist.

Perfectionists also measure their value according to how they're treated by those closest to them. For example, if the perfectionist's spouse is loving, tender, and attentive, it enhances his or her sense of self-worth. If his or her spouse is indifferent, insensitive, or distracted, it diminishes his or her sense of self-worth.

That's a lot of pressure to place on someone. Over time, it can become intensely frustrating to that individual, provoking and stoking feelings of resentment.

Here's a promise: when you learn to silence your inner critic, your relationships will noticeably improve.

#12 - IT MAKES YOU SUSCEPTIBLE TO THE PEOPLE-PLEASING HABIT

~

Perfectionists have difficulty saying no to people. They not only put constant pressure on themselves to meet unreasonable standards, but also aim to please others along the way. They measure their self-worth by their achievements, but look toward others to *validate* those achievements. If their efforts result in others' approval, they feel happy and valuable. If others express disapproval or disappointment, they feel inadequate.

They only feel good enough when their friends, family members, coworkers, and bosses praise them.

This mindset is rooted in insecurity. Perfectionists are driven to be flawless, in part, to avoid criticism. They want people to think of them as useful and reliable. So they go to great lengths to please everyone around them, usually by striving for perfection.

Recall from earlier that people who exhibit perfectionistic behavior loathe uncertainty. Changing circumstances and new situations make them feel vulnerable. If they can't be sure their actions will result in success, they'd rather not act at all.

In this light, the attempt to please others is used as a mechanism to mitigate the fear of failure. If the perfectionist is able to gain others' approval, the uncertainty of a situation is easier to tolerate. And in the perfectionist's mind, the most effective way to please others is to cater to their wishes and be flawless in the process.

The inability to say no carries consequences. We put other people's priorities ahead of our own, ignoring our needs and goals. We spend our time and energy accommodating others to the point that we have nothing left in the tank for ourselves. Meanwhile, we inadvertently train those around us to take us for granted.

This predicament only exacerbates the people-pleasing habit in perfectionists. The more we put others ahead of ourselves, the more we try to be who they *want* us to be. This is one of the self-destructive side effects of seeking external validation.

Coming Up Next...

You're now fully aware of the many ways perfectionism

can adversely impact your career, relationships, and overall quality of life. In *Part II: 10 Signs Your Perfectionism Is Out Of Control*, I'll show you how to gauge the extent of the problem.

PART II

10 SIGNS YOUR PERFECTIONISM IS OUT OF CONTROL

∾

Everyone has an inner critic. It's a niggling voice that persistently calls attention to our inadequacies, and in the process gives rise to perpetual doubt, guilt, and shame.

Most people have managed to dull its bite. They've managed to suppress their inner critics so the hyper-judgmental voice has little impact on their ability to get things done.

Some have even managed to ignore it altogether.

But not perfectionists. Perfectionists are constantly at the mercy of this disparaging voice. It continuously berates them, claiming they're not skilled enough, not smart enough, not good enough, and not worth liking.

It asserts they fail to measure up.

Some perfectionists are able to manage this voice. They're able to live their lives despite the persistent nagging about their failings and weaknesses. For other perfectionists, their inner critic is a nonstop aggravation. It's an ever-present stumbling block that diminishes their productivity and belittles their sense of achievement.

Their perfectionism is out of control.

In the following pages, we're going to gauge the severity of your perfectionistic behavior. If any of the following traits sound familiar to you, it's time to take corrective action. Your self-confidence, success, and long-term happiness are at stake.

SIGN #1 - FAILURE TO ACHIEVE YOUR GOALS CAUSES YOU TO BECOME DEPRESSED

~

Each of us has expectations. We anticipate particular outcomes whenever we take action. When reality fails to measure up to our predictions, we experience disappointment.

This is a natural response when we act in the face of uncertainty. With time, our disappointment dissipates and we're able to get on with our lives.

Perfectionists have more difficulty recovering from missed expectations. They process their disappointing circumstances more negatively than others. To that end, their disappointment is sometimes so severe that it's a precursor to depression.

It's worth noting that I'm not referring to clinical depression, a condition diagnosed according to criteria listed in the *Diagnostic and Statistical Manual of Mental Disorders* (DSM-5). Rather, I'm referring to *situational* depression. This is a short-term state during which your mood and self-esteem plummet, and you find yourself unable to adapt to your situation.

Failing to achieve goals is a part of life. No one achieves every goal they set for themselves. The important thing is how we deal with the failure.

A healthy approach is to learn from it, to use it as constructive feedback for personal growth. This mindset is intrinsic to a quote made by retired basketball player Michael Jordan:

> *I've missed more than 9000 shots in my career. I've lost almost 300 games. 26 times, I've been trusted to take the game winning shot and missed. I've failed over and over and over again in my life. And this is why I succeed."*

An unhealthy approach, often seen in perfectionists, is to perceive failure as proof of inadequacy. Rather than learn from failure, hardcore perfectionists allow it to shape their sense of self-worth. No effort is made to use the situation as a learning experience. Consequently, their disappointment festers, ultimately making them feel miserable and dejected.

This is no way to live! If failing to meet goals makes you feel depressed, it may indicate your perfectionism is out of control.

SIGN #2 - SUCCESS RARELY, IF EVER, BRINGS YOU JOY

~

Have you ever done something well, and then chided yourself over an insignificant detail? Perfectionists do this to themselves over and over. And it prevents them from feeling any sense of true accomplishment. An outcome most people would celebrate as a success leaves the perfectionist feeling morose. They focus on the tiny detail that got away from them.

An example is a student who receive an "A" on a test, and then scolds himself because he failed to get a perfect score.

Or consider the executive who gives a stellar presentation to her bosses, and then berates herself for neglecting to include a particular speaking point.

Another example: the novelist who writes a bestselling

book only to chastise himself over the pacing of a particular scene.

Diehard perfectionists are uncompromising. They
measure their worth based on what they *failed* to do rather
than what they *succeeded* in doing. For this reason, they
rarely, if ever, experience the joy and sense of accomplishment that comes from a job well done.

This isn't to say the perfectionist is unable to recognize,
or acknowledge, success. On the contrary, he or she *expects*
it. The problem is, imperfect results conflict with his or her
archetypal self. Small, inconsequential mistakes feel like
major failures. This triggers self-criticism.

Consequently, the perfectionist is unable to take pleasure in results that are "good," or even "great." The results
must be flawless for him or her to feel satisfied. Unfortunately, because flawlessness is rare - and sporadic in the
best of cases - the perfectionist consigns himself or herself
to a perpetual state is discontent.

Consider your own experience. Do you have difficulty
taking pride in your work due to minor errors? Do you ever
feel inadequate, even when everyone around you sings your
praises? Have you ever felt devastated over a perceived
failure despite others commending you on a job well done?

If so, it's time to rein in your rigid, unforgiving perfectionistic tendencies.

SIGN #3 - YOU'RE ALWAYS LOOKING FOR THINGS YOU DID WRONG RATHER THAN CELEBRATING THINGS YOU DID RIGHT

∼

This habit follows from the previous one. In the previous section, we talked about the tendency to focus on minor faults to the point that you're unable to take pleasure in your successes. Here, you're actively *looking* for such faults in everything you do, even when they're unnoticeable to others.

You strive for flawlessness. But you instinctively recognize that flawlessness is a mirage. It's an unrealistic standard, and one that's impossible to maintain. Give that, you assume you've made errors. So you look for them, convinced they're present and waiting to be found.

This habit inevitably leads toward a downward spiral. For once you identify *one* fault in your performance, you're naturally driven to look for others.

Worse, each fault you identify sets off another round of self-recrimination. You lambaste yourself, certain that you could have performed better, made wiser decisions, or achieved more than you achieved.

It's one thing for us to examine our mistakes, and look for ways to improve our performance. That's the path toward personal and professional growth. In most cases, growth is continuous and incremental. It's an ongoing process.

It's another thing entirely to look for mistakes, use them as confirmation of our inadequacies, and reprimand ourselves accordingly.

The growth-minded individual recognizes that imperfect results stemming from his or her mistakes are merely feedback. They show him or her how to perform more effectively in the future. This person can reflect on the mistakes, and move forward with confidence.

The unyielding perfectionist has an entirely different perspective. He or she is disinterested toward effecting ongoing, incremental growth. Instead, the perfectionistic individual considers flawlessness to be the only goal worth pursuing. Anything less is a failure.

The perfectionist is highly critical of mistakes, regardless of their size and import. Minor faults are as glaring and intolerable as major faults. Because the perfectionist is always looking for them (and certain to find them), his or her perceived failure is a forgone conclusion.

Here's the good news: once you learn to curb your

inner perfectionist, you'll stop looking for mistakes and using them as evidence of your shortcomings. Instead, you'll see them as learning opportunities that help you to become a better version of yourself.

SIGN #4 - YOU BECOME DEFENSIVE WHEN OTHERS HIGHLIGHT ERRORS YOU'VE MADE

~

Nobody looks forward to criticism. It showcases our mistakes and shortcomings. When someone critiques something we've done or created, it's difficult to resist taking negative comments personally.

In fact, we have psychological defense mechanisms to deal with criticism. These mechanisms help us to keep our anxiety levels in check when others' comments threaten our egos.

For example, a high-school student, when told by his teacher that he's capable of doing better work, might respond, *"I didn't have enough time on this assignment!"*

A salesperson, when informed by her manager that she's failing to hit her sales targets, might counter, *"I can't convert low-quality leads!"*

Upon hearing his or her child complain that dinner is too salty, a parent might retort, *"If you think it's so easy, cook your own dinner!"*

In other words, we become defensive. Most people recognize when they're being overly defensive, and take corrective measures to rein themselves in.

But not perfectionists.

Perfectionists take defensiveness to an entirely new level. They perceive negative comments as accusations regarding their worth. They're quick to defend themselves because they perceive doing so as a matter of survival. In the perfectionist's mind, negative comments are an indictment of ineptitude, and threaten to reveal him or her as worthless.

I know this from experience.

Before I learned to silence my inner critic, I was hyper-defensive. If someone noted that my timing was off while playing the guitar, I'd blame the drummer. If one of my teachers pointed out that I wasn't doing my best work, I'd blame others students for distracting me. If my boss observed an error in one of my reports, I'd blame someone else for not providing the data I needed.

These reactions are embarrassing to admit (and they're just the tip of the proverbial iceberg). But looking back, it's clear to me that my defensiveness, while an inherent component of my perfectionism, was borne out of feelings of inadequacy, shame, and guilt. I couldn't tolerate criticism because it always felt like an allegation of impotence.

If you can relate, stick with me. I'm going to show you

how to curb your perfectionistic temperament, and deal
with criticism in a healthy manner.

SIGN #5 - YOU CONSIDER ASKING FOR HELP TO BE A SIGN OF WEAKNESS

∽

This attitude isn't the exclusive domain of perfectionists. Many people are unwilling to ask for help, fearful they'll appear unknowledgeable, unskilled, or incompetent. They'd rather struggle on their own than reveal their limitations.

But for perfectionists, asking for help is a more serious matter. It underscores their inability to perform. It's an admission that they're ineffectual.

This type of concession is unacceptable to perfection-istic individuals. They view their performance as a measure of their worth. If they're unable to perform without others' assistance, they see themselves as failures.

This chain of reasoning seems nonsensical to non-perfectionists. But recall that perfectionists see things in black and white. They harbor an all-or-nothing attitude. To that end, they evaluate their performance according to a rigid succeed-or-fail yardstick.

There is no middle ground.

If they need help, they perceive that need to be evidence of their inadequacy. Because the perfectionist's personal worth is wrapped up in his or her obsession with flawlessness, this mindset instinctively provokes feelings of shame and guilt.

When I used to have a corporate job, I was responsible for creating a report used to analyze the flow of funds (I won't bore you with the details). This task required that I write code to pull data from multiple databases. I took pride in knowing how to do this, and being able to do it without mistakes.

But on occasion, I'd run into problems. The data in the report were inaccurate, which implied my coding was bad.

My team had a coding expert. He could write clean, effective code in a fraction of the time I needed to do the same. But I refused to ask him for help. Asking for help was an indignity. A humiliation. It would have meant admitting that I was imperfect, a concession I considered an embarrassment.

So I'd spend hours tweaking my code to get it to work properly when a resolution was a single phone call away.

That was my inner perfectionist at work. I was doing everything I could to avoid having to ask for help. I didn't want to appear weak or admit to myself that I was unable to measure up to my too-lofty standards.

It was only after I curbed my perfectionistic behavior that I realized asking for help isn't a sign of weakness. On the contrary, it's a sign of strength. It shows that you recognize the value of collaboration, a smoother and quicker path toward personal and professional growth.

If you're seldom willing to ask for assistance, ask yourself whether it's because you want to appear perfect. If that's the reason, it's time to get a handle on your perfectionism.

SIGN #6 - YOU REFUSE TO DELEGATE OR OUTSOURCE BECAUSE YOU MUST BE IN CONTROL

~

Perfectionists like to stay in control. They *need* to stay in control. The moment they hand over the reins to someone else, they feel vulnerable.

There are three reasons.

First, perfectionists are highly motivated to make sure tasks are done faultlessly. They feel that if a job isn't done correctly, there's no reason to do it at all. They also feel that mistakes are avoidable and therefore inexcusable.

Second, perfectionists have confidence in their ability to perform flawlessly. Importantly, they don't feel the same way about others. Perhaps you've heard someone mutter, *"If you want something done right, you have to do it yourself."* There's a good chance that person was a perfectionist.

Third, perfectionists feel that delegating work diminishes their importance. They feel valued based on their knowledge and skills. They believe that delegating tasks to others will result in their being upstaged by those to whom they delegate. This is the reason some managers remain subject matter experts when they arguably should pass the baton to qualified subordinates.

When my perfectionistic behavior was out of control, I was a control freak. This wasn't a coincidence. The former encouraged the latter.

While attending high school and college, I hated working on group projects. I needed to be in control because I was convinced that I was the most capable person in the room (hubris was my constant companion).

While playing guitar in a garage band, I needed to be in command. I considered myself the most skilled musician present (humility wasn't my strong suit), and believed I deserved to call the shots.

While in Corporate America, I cringed at the prospect of working on projects with my coworkers. Since my name would appear on the projects, I felt justified in exerting overt influence on how the projects were handled.

I look back at my behavior and recoil. It's amazing that I had friends in high school and college. It's a wonder my bandmates put up with me. And I'm still uncertain how my coworkers tolerated me on project after project.

Put simply, my perfectionistic tendencies ran rampant. Fortunately, I found that curbing my perfectionism was the key to subduing my inner control freak.

SIGN #7 - YOU'RE UNABLE TO MOVE FORWARD AFTER MAKING MISTAKES

~

M istakes are an essential building block for personal development. They guide us, letting us know how we can improve our performance. They enhance our problem solving and critical thinking skills. Mistakes give us opportunities to make connections between ideas, and deepen our knowledge and appreciation of concepts.

And importantly, when we make mistakes, regardless of size and consequence, we become less fearful of being wrong down the road. We become increasingly desensitized to our inner critics.

Perfectionists seldom enjoy these benefits. As we noted earlier, they obsess over mistakes, perceiving them as evidence of failure and inadequacy. Rather than contemplating their faulty decisions and avoidable errors, and using them to inform their growth, they berate themselves.

The magnitude and significance of a mistake doesn't matter to the perfectionist. The mere fact that a mistake was made is vexing to him or her.

Here's an example from my own life:

I used to micromanage myself when meeting new people. From my initial handshake and greeting to my facial expressions and conversational skills, everything had to be perfect. When something was off - for instance, my handshake was less firm than I intended or my lack of eye contact caused the other person to become disinterested in furthering the conversation - I'd chide myself over it later.

I failed to use such blunders as learning opportunities. Instead, I used them as opportunities to scold myself. Consequently, interpersonal interactions became a constant source of stress.

I had difficulty moving forward.

It's not just personal mistakes that exasperate perfectionists. They find others' mistakes similarly vexing. Here again, the size and significance of an error are irrelevant. People with perfectionistic leanings are highly critical of even the smallest details that fail to meet their standards.

Worse, it's not enough for perfectionists that others correct their mistakes. Their opinions of the individuals are already tainted. Remember, perfectionists see things in black and white. Good or bad. Succeed or fail. Perfect or useless.

I mentioned earlier that I was difficult to be around

years ago. My perfectionism prompted disagreeable behavior (that's a diplomatic way of putting it). While some of this behavior was focused inward, much of it was focused on other people. I couldn't move past my own mistakes. And I couldn't move past theirs.

If you can relate to this problem, I have good news. Mistakes, yours and others, will seem far less consequential once you learn to silence your inner perfectionist.

SIGN #8 - YOU'RE OFTEN PARALYZED WITH INDECISION OR INACTION

~

I n *Part I: 12 Ways Perfectionism Negatively Impacts Your Life*, we noted that perfectionists are highly averse to taking risks. To them, risk signifies potential failure, an unacceptable outcome. Consequently, when faced with a risky proposition, they're waylaid by indecision and lethargy.

Sometimes, this response - or more accurately, this *non-*response - is a form of procrastination. The perfectionist puts off making a decision or taking action until circumstances align in a way that guarantees success.

Other times, the response is an avoidance tactic designed to dodge a particular decision or activity. The perfectionist uses this tactic to avoid situations that might expose him or her to unpredictable outcomes. Here, the perfectionist's goal isn't to merely *delay* making a decision or taking action. It's to avoid doing so altogether.

This motivation stems from the perfectionist's awareness that he or she isn't the best in a particular situation.

For example, a student might excel in math, but lag behind her peers in reading comprehension. Thus, she's quick to participate in class discussions involving the former, but clams up when the latter subject is broached.

Another example is the salesperson who feels comfortable pitching products to prospective customers, but awkward and tense when presenting ideas to his bosses and coworkers. Accordingly, he has no problem cold calling and pitching strangers, but does everything in his power to avoid giving in-house presentations.

Or consider the athletic, yet perfectionistic, individual who performs flawlessly on the basketball court, but less admirably on the tennis court. As a result, she jumps at the chance to play basketball, but refuses outright to play tennis.

Indecisiveness and inertia are the perfectionist's natural reaction to "risky" situations. When faced with uncertainty, he or she either suffers from "paralysis by analysis" or simply refuses to act. The alternative, making decisions and taking action when circumstances are suboptimal, is intolerable to the perfectionist.

One of the downsides to having this reaction is that perfectionists never build resilience against imperfect results. Nor do they learn the valuable lessons inherent in taking risks. Finally, perfectionistic individuals seldom experience significant personal and professional growth because they rarely venture outside their comfort zones.

They excel in their areas of speciality. But their indecision and lethargy in the face of uncertainty hobble their development in other areas.

SIGN #9 - OTHERS FIND YOU DIFFICULT TO WORK WITH BECAUSE YOU WANT THINGS DONE IN A PARTICULAR WAY

∾

I mentioned earlier that perfectionists need to be in control. It's in their nature. The alternative is to give up control to others, and in the process leave themselves exposed to unpredictable outcomes.

In group projects, perfectionists often take the lead and maintain control as a way to reduce their anxiety. The more they feel in control, the less concerned they are with potential failure. The moment they lose (or surrender) control is the moment they feel vulnerable.

This attitude makes perfectionists difficult to work with. They're convinced their way is the best way, and consequently dismiss others' ideas. In reality, their desire for control springs from their insecurities. They fear showing weaknesses or flaws.

Perfectionists exert control to try to minimize the degree of uncertainty inherent in group efforts. The only way they feel doing so is possible is by commandeering projects. This endeavor manifests in one of two ways.

In some cases, the perfectionist insists on doing everything him or herself. That way, he or she can ensure flawlessness.

In other cases, the perfectionist will allow others to contribute, but micromanage every step of the process. He or she will loom over other participants, closely inspecting their work. The motivation is the same as above: to ensure flawlessness.

Micromanaging people causes them to feel frustrated, distrustful, and resentful. It lowers their morale, hampers their productivity, and saps their motivation and initiative. Ultimately, it causes people to dread working with the micromanager.

As a recovering perfectionist, I speak from experience. I'm ashamed to say that I've lost count of the number of people I've driven crazy with my perfectionistic attitude and consequent desire for control. I'm mortified when I recall how difficult I was to work with.

I wanted things done in a particular way, and with rare exceptions it was my way or no way at all.

Controlling my perfectionistic behavior allowed me to finally let go of this irksome personality trait.

SIGN #10 - YOU HAVE DIFFICULTY FINISHING PROJECTS

∽

Perfectionists have a tough time completing their work. They aim for flawlessness, which seems admirable to the casual observer. But we know better. The pursuit of flawlessness is a constant obstacle to project completion. There's always room for improvement, and thus projects are never quite finished.

This is a serious problem for uncompromising perfectionists. If they feel their work can be improved, they're inclined to keep working on it. But of course, there are consequences.

For executives, it might entail turning projects in late. For students, it could involve spending twice as much time on assignments, losing sleep and personal time in the process. For novelists, it may mean taking years to finally publish their books.

There's always an aspect that can be refined. There's always a detail that can be improved. There's always an edit that can be made.

Ultimately, projects started by perfectionists often languish in a type of purgatory.

Many perfectionists fail to *start* their work at all. This reluctance to take action may stem from a perceived lack of skill or time.

For example, an executive who obsesses over being flawless may be unwilling to start working on a presentation if he hasn't yet mastered PowerPoint.

A student burdened with a perfectionistic disposition might refuse to start working on a class project because she lacks the requisite materials.

A novelist who aspires to be perfect may have difficulty starting a new book if he's unable to come up with a superb opening scene.

A homeowner predisposed toward perfection might delay cleaning her house if she lacks the time to do the job in its entirety, from floor to ceiling.

In the end, tasks are never finished. Projects are never started. Ideas are never acted upon. And goals are left unrealized. The perfectionist's all-or-nothing mindset prevents him or her from completing work, or discourages him or her from starting it at all.

POP QUIZ: HOW SEVERE IS YOUR PERFECTIONISM?

~

I n the section *Perfectionism: A Recipe For Unhappiness*, I asserted that everyone has an inner perfectionist. Most folks have learned to control this highly judgmental part of their psyche. They're able to ignore the voice that relentlessly criticizes their efforts and points accusingly at their shortcomings.

Because you're reading this book, it's a safe guess that you have yet to reach that point. You know you're a perfectionist and recognize that your perfectionism is taking a serious toll. It's hampering your career, hurting your relationships, and destroying your productivity.

In short, it's negatively affecting your quality of life.

We're going to gauge the severity of the problem.

Below, you'll find 10 statements, each of which is an indication of perfectionism.

Here's what I'd like you to do: decide the extent to which each statement describes you. Indicate its accuracy by assigning a number from one to five. One signifies the statement is completely untrue. Five means it's spot on.

After you've "rated" each of the 10 statements, we'll add up your score. Your final tally will reveal whether your perfectionism is out of control.

1. I'm only satisfied with my work when it's perfect.
2. I thrive on validation from others, and feel discouraged when my efforts fail to draw praise.
3. I'd rather do nothing than do something imperfectly.
4. I have a hard time making decisions and taking action when faced with uncertainty.
5. I dislike working in groups because I'm unable to ensure everything is done flawlessly.
6. I must always be in control, and feel anxious and uncomfortable when I'm not.
7. I never ask for help because it makes me feel incompetent.
8. I constantly correct people, pointing out their mistakes (even trivial ones).
9. I abandon projects when I suspect the results will be less than perfect.
10. When I look back on my life, I see a past filled

with failures and mistakes rather than successes and reasons to celebrate.

Let's add up your score, and use it to determine the severity of your perfectionism.

1 to 15 points - You have your inner perfectionist well under control. You can hear the small voice in your head trying to convince you that you're not good enough. But you have no trouble ignoring it. You may not be in dire need of the tactics found in *The Joy Of Imperfection*. But this book will help you to understand the struggles of other perfectionists.

16 to 30 points - Your perfectionistic behavior influences your outlook and interactions with others. It's not a severe problem, but sometimes causes you unnecessary anxiety. It's also hampering your personal and professional development in small, but obtrusive ways.

31 to 40 points - Your perfectionism has a major impact on your sense of self-worth. Your inner critic is intolerant of mistakes and failures, and repeatedly berates you for both. You're unable to accept praise at face value because you feel your work can always be better.

41 to 50 points - You constantly feel stressed, anxious, discouraged, and even depressed. You never feel good enough or smart enough. Everything you do evokes self-recrimination, and triggers feelings of doubt, shame, and guilt. Your perfectionism is making you miserable.

The Bottom Line

If your perfectionistic behavior is negatively affecting your life, you'll find the advice in the following pages to be invaluable. In *Part III: A Complete Action Plan For Overcoming Perfectionism*, I'll show you how to finally silence your inner critic for good.

Keep in mind, the effort to quell your perfectionism is a marathon, not a sprint. It'll take time, commitment, and dedication. The good news is that if you stick with it, you *will* succeed.

I guarantee it.

Coming Up Next...

I'm going to give you more than a dozen tactics and exercises designed to desensitize your inner critic. Once you incorporate them into your daily experience, you'll find that the judgmental voice in your head will grow quieter. Eventually, you won't even be able to hear it.

PART III

A COMPLETE ACTION PLAN FOR OVERCOMING PERFECTIONISM

~

I've found that with any type of personal development, the most effective path forward is to make slow, incremental progress. New habits are easier to form and more likely to last when you give your brain time to acclimate to them.

Going slowly will also make it easier to recover from the occasional, inevitable stumbles. Missteps seem less consequential when the steps are small.

Be patient with yourself. If you stumble, forgive yourself. Perfectionism is a difficult mindset to overcome. Perfectionistic habits are difficult to break, especially if you've developed and reinforced them over a lifetime.

Think of the following plan as a personal training regimen. But rather than training your body, we're going to train (or retrain) your mind.

I promise the effort will be worthwhile because there's so much at stake. Obsessing about being perfect invariably leads to chronic unhappiness, and that informs your quality of life.

The good news is that you're on the cusp of making a radical, positive transformation. With time, you'll experience the marvelous freedom of being able make decisions and take action without fear of failure and self-recrimination.

One last note: each of the following sections includes an exercise. The exercises are designed to reinforce the ideas and tactics covered throughout *Part III*. I strongly encourage you to do them, even if a few seem silly.

Now, let's roll up our sleeves and get started!

REALIZE PERFECTION IS AN ILLUSION

~

There's no such thing as "perfect." It follows that striving to be perfect in all things is a fool's errand. While flawlessness may be possible in short spurts, it's little more than an illusion over the long run.

No one can maintain such a rigid standard. That's why perfectionists often struggle with high stress levels, along with persistent feelings of disappointment, guilt, and shame.

The first step toward recovery is to recognize the illusory nature of perfectionism.

Being perfect requires being in control of all situations, circumstances, and conditions at all times. The problem is, such absolute control is impossible. It's a false expectation.

Most situations impose a degree of uncertainty. This uncertainty has the potential to delay, hamper, or otherwise obstruct the best-laid plans.

Being perfect also requires avoiding making mistakes. This too is impossible over the long run. Mistakes are an inevitable part of the human condition. Life is about screwing up and learning from our screw-ups. Show me a person who makes zero mistakes and I'll show you a person who experiences zero personal and professional growth.

Once you recognize that perfectionism is an illusion, you'll find it easier to muzzle your inner critic. When that voice is silenced, you'll see your pursuit of flawlessness for what it truly is: a way to avoid criticism and recrimination, from yourself and others.

EXERCISE #1

RECALL the last time you tried to be perfect.

Perhaps it was while giving a presentation to a prospective client. Maybe it was while playing basketball with your friends. Perhaps it was while cooking a meal for your family.

Next, think of the many ways you lacked absolute control over the situation.

For example, you weren't in control of your prospective client's mood. Maybe he was having a terrible day, and thus was less than receptive to your presentation.

You weren't in control of your teammates. Perhaps one

or more were dealing with muscle soreness that impacted their performance.

And while cooking a meal might give you the sense that you're in control, it's easy to make mistakes. You might use too much salt or cook on too-high heat. Or the person you're cooking for might arrive late, allowing the meal to cool.

This exercise is designed to increase your awareness that you have less control over your circumstances than you might imagine. And without absolute control, perfection is a pipe dream.

ACKNOWLEDGE THAT PURSUING PERFECTION IS HARMFUL

~

Many people joke about being perfectionists. For example, a student might quip, "*I never turn assignments in on time because I'm a perfectionist.*" A chef might jest, "*My dishes take a long time to prepare because I ensure they're perfect before they leave my kitchen.*"

Some people delight in calling themselves perfectionists. For example, a job candidate might claim, "*My biggest weakness is that I'm a perfectionist,*" hoping the interviewer will consider this weakness to be a strength.

Both tendencies ignore the harmful effects associated with true perfectionism.

For example, consider your relationships. If you regularly obsess over being perfect, your unrealistic standards have almost certainly impacted others, tainting their perception of you. Your friends, family members, business partners, coworkers, and significant others have probably felt hurt, resentful, or frustrated at various points.

Consider your productivity. Perfectionistic behavior prevents you from getting things done. Tasks take too long to complete. Projects never get finished. Why? Because there's always room for improvement.

Consider your mental health. You know from experience that trying to be perfect leads to increased stress, greater anxiety, shame and guilt, and feelings of personal failure. As noted earlier, multiple studies show that perfectionism is linked to depression and suicidal thoughts.

Consider your personal and professional development. Perfectionistic individuals take fewer risks. They stay within their comfort zones, where it's safe. Unfortunately, doing so stunts their growth.

Recognizing the harmful effects of perfectionism is essential to overcoming the obsession. It's a reminder of what's at stake. Once you link your perfectionistic tendencies to a notable decline in your quality of life, you'll become more willing to do the work toward making a positive change.

EXERCISE #2

THINK ABOUT specific instances in the recent past when your perfectionism adversely affected your life.

For example, did you recently anger your spouse or

partner by holding him or her to an unreasonably high standard? Did you frustrate a friend by clinging to unrealistic expectations?

Did your perfectionism recently cause you to become indecisive and lethargic at your job? Did it compel you to procrastinate on important projects?

Have you recently experienced exasperation and increased stress due to your intolerance for mistakes? Have you allowed your inner critic to lambast you repeatedly for perceived failures?

Do you get the feeling your personal life and/or career are stagnating due to your aversion to risk? Do you feel that you're not growing?

Write down every negative impact related to your perfectionistic behavior.

Alcoholics in recovery are encouraged to think about how their addiction is interfering with their lives. The idea is that recognizing the harmful effects will motivate the recovering alcoholic to treat therapy seriously.

This exercise makes use of the same tactic. It reveals how perfectionism is adversely affecting your life, so you'll be highly motivated to overcome it.

GET USED TO DECONSTRUCTING YOUR INNER CRITIC

~

Your inner critic has an entitlement complex. This complex stems from years of having its voice heard, and then observing its influence on your thoughts, actions, and self-image.

In short, your inner critic has learned to expect you to take its criticism at face value.

For this reason alone, it's important that you learn to deconstruct its claims. Each time your inner critic castigates you, ask yourself whether its assertions are valid. Can you trust them?

(Spoiler: no, you can't.)

For example, suppose you're planning to give a presentation to coworkers at your workplace. You know the material well and are well-prepared. But you're nervous.

Although your last presentation went well, it wasn't perfect. Mistakes were made.

Predictably, your inner critic will take the opportunity to highlight that fact. It'll tell you that you're inept. It'll try to convince you that you're not sufficiently knowledgeable to speak with authority. It'll weave a future narrative in which you're the target of ridicule and derision from your coworkers.

Now, stop a moment and deconstruct your inner critic's claims and criticism.

First, is it true that you're inept? Almost certainly not. You've given presentations before. Perhaps they were less than perfect, but does that matter? Remember, perfection is an unreasonable standard.

Your inner critic's veracity is already in question.

Second, is it true that you lack sufficient knowledge to give the presentation? Absolutely not. You're familiar with the material. And you're well-prepared to explain it to your coworkers.

That's another blow to your inner critic's power.

Third, how likely is it that your coworkers will ridicule you following your presentation? The idea is preposterous. Your coworkers are more likely to admire your courage and expertise on the topic.

That's strike three for your inner critic.

By deconstructing its claims, you'll reveal them as fallacious. And once the truth is out, your inner critic will have less influence over you. You'll recognize that its assertions are groundless.

EXERCISE #3

REFLEXIVE DECONSTRUCTION TAKES PRACTICE. Like any habit, it's developed through consistent action. You've spent years listening to your inner critic, assuming its assertions were true. Learning to instinctively question them will require rewiring your brain.

Let's start right now.

The next time your inner critic rears its head and criticizes you, challenge it. Scrutinize every claim, one by one. Strip away all falsehoods and evaluate the leftovers.

You'll discover that your inner critic cannot be trusted. Once this fact becomes clear, you'll be able to disregard it with confidence.

GIVE YOURSELF PERMISSION TO MAKE MISTAKES

~

M istakes are the bane of perfectionists. They're evidence of the perfectionist's perceived inadequacies, and therefore invoke self-criticism and negative self-talk. This, as we've noted, ultimately triggers feelings of guilt and shame.

Most perfectionists try to avoid making mistakes at all costs. Unfortunately, this effort does more harm than good. It not only reinforces perfectionistic behavior, but it also hampers growth. After all, the only way to avoid making mistakes is to remain within one's comfort zone.

Mistakes are a valuable learning tool. They reveal cognitive biases, errors in judgment, and procedural inefficiencies. They teach us about ourselves, and serve as a reality check against our misguided assumptions.

In short, mistakes fuel our growth in skills and knowledge, and in doing so make life more rewarding. As acclaimed playwright George Bernard Shaw once noted, *"a life spent making mistakes is not only more honorable, but more useful than a life spent doing nothing."*

It's important to give yourself permission to make mistakes, to make errors in judgment, and even to fail. At the very least, you'll benefit from valuable feedback regarding what works and what doesn't work in various situations. You'll also experience less anxiety about your decisions and performance.

Of course, giving yourself this type of latitude is easier said than done, especially if you're a lifelong perfectionist. For this reason, I strongly recommend doing the following exercise.

EXERCISE #4

CONSIDER a task you'd like to undertake. Grab a piece of paper and write down a list of the potential mistakes you might make while working on it. Next, go down the list and imagine the worst possible consequence of each mistake. You'll find they're less serious than you might envision.

For example, let's say you'd like to plan a vacation for you and your spouse. Following are some possible gaffes you might make in the process:

- You fail to choose the "perfect" destination.

- You fail to reserve accommodations at a "perfect" hotel.
- You fail to purchase flight tickets on the "perfect" airline.
- You fail to make dinner reservations at "perfect" restaurants.

What's the worst possible outcome of choosing an imperfect destination? You and your spouse will still have a rewarding experience. You'll still enjoy each other's company away from the stresses and pressures of normal daily life. After all, it's still a vacation.

What's the worst that can happen if you fail to book a room at a "perfect" hotel? The hotel you *do* stay at will probably be just as comfortable and enjoyable.

What's the worst possible consequence of failing to fly on a "perfect" airline (if there *is* such a thing)? Perhaps you won't receive a snack. Maybe you won't receive five-star service. But the flight is still bound to be comfortable (or at least tolerable), and you'll probably reach your destination at the expected arrival time.

What's the worst that can happen if you fail to reserve tables at the best restaurants? You're not going to starve. On the contrary, most vacation destinations offer a plethora of high-quality restaurants. You and your spouse will be able to dine in style regardless.

This exercise underscores the fact that mistakes have less-serious consequences than we presume. They can, in fact, help us to become more adaptive to circumstances that lie beyond our control.

GIVE YOURSELF PERMISSION TO
BE WRONG

~

No one likes to be wrong. It's a difficult circumstance for most of us to accept. We're emotionally invested in our opinions, decisions, and actions, and being wrong is a blow to our egos.

Think back to the last time you made a statement that was challenged by someone. Did you get defensive? Did you "double down" on your statement, prompted by a fear of criticism rather than confidence and conviction?

I can relate. I used to do it all of the time. I couldn't tolerate being wrong because it meant my perception of self-worth, predicated on my being *right*, was faulty.

In a word, I was persnickety. And any indication that someone believed I was wrong would trigger my defensiveness.

Does this sound familiar? Can you relate?

Fear of being wrong is a common attribute among perfectionists. And it's one that not only leads to unnecessary confrontations, but also increased stress, low self-esteem, and self-condemnation.

Realize that being wrong isn't a reflection of your skills, knowledge, or morality. Nor is it a reflection of your value. It simply means an opinion you hold is inaccurate, or an action you've taken was misguided.

These are learning opportunities.

When you give yourself permission to be wrong, you allow yourself to grow from these opportunities. You begin to care less about maintaining a facade of absolute correctness, and care *more* about rectifying unsound positions and bad habits.

Admitting that you're wrong isn't easy. As a perfectionist, it can be downright uncomfortable. But the more you do it, the easier it gets. Eventually, the possibility of being wrong will hold no fear over you whatsoever.

EXERCISE #5

THE NEXT TIME someone challenges something you've said, ask for clarification. Seek to understand the challenge, and then evaluate it rationally. Be willing to cede ground if the challenge is valid.

If your statement is fact-based, it should be easy to verify whether the challenge is correct or incorrect.

For example, suppose you tell a friend, "*The movie starts at 7:00.*"

Your friend counters, "*No, it doesn't. It starts at 7:20.*"

It's easy to confirm whether your friend's claim is correct. If it is, apologize and move on.

If the statement you've made stems from an opinion, correctness is more difficult to gauge. Even so, recognize the validity of the challenger's opinion, even if you disagree with it.

For example, suppose you tell your friend, "*That was a wonderful movie.*"

Your friend counters, "*That movie was terrible.*"

Rather than becoming defensive, ask your friend to explain his perspective. If his arguments are reasonable, acknowledge as much. Then, either adjust your opinion in light of his arguments, or agree to disagree, and move on.

If you always insist that you're right, your brain will resist any efforts you make to admit you're wrong. But as noted above, it gets easier with time and repetition. Once you wear down your brain's resistance, you'll be able to admit to being wrong without harming your self-esteem or sense of self-worth.

LOWER YOUR UNREASONABLY HIGH STANDARDS

∼

As a perfectionist, you probably set impractical standards of achievement for yourself. You're not alone. All of us do so. It's a part of our credo.

Unrealistic standards would be less self-defeating if perfectionists could tolerate their inability to meet them. Sadly, they can't. When their performances fails to meet the standards they've imposed upon themselves, they judge themselves too harshly. They open themselves to negative self-talk, allowing their inner critics to chastise them.

The result? Their self-confidence and sense of self-worth take a beating. Worse, they become even less receptive to taking risks, adopting goal-avoidance behaviors.

Unattainable standards are a recipe for disappointment, guilt, and shame. If your sense of worth is intrinsically tethered to your ability to meet impossible demands, you'll always feel frustrated and inadequate.

The good news is, it's easy to adjust this aspect of your perfectionistic behavior. Simply replace your impossible standards with realistic ones.

This practice, demonstrated in the exercise below, is straightforward. In fact, it may seem overly simplistic. The upside is that once you replace your impractical standards with achievable ones, you'll be less vulnerable to the judgmental voice of your inner critic.

EXERCISE #6

THINK about a task you're planning to undertake today. Write down the criteria by which you gauge the success of completing the task.

For example, suppose you're planning to clean your home. You intend to wash the windows, vacuum and mop the floors, dust the furniture, clean out the refrigerator, wipe off the countertops, and scrub down the bathrooms.

Now, take a sheet a paper and divide it into two columns. Write down your benchmarks for "success" in the left column.

For example, you might want your windows to be literally spotless. You may want your floors to glisten as if new. You might want the wood surfaces of your furniture to shine as if recently finished with a wax polish.

Writing these things down may seem unnatural and awkward. That's understandable. Most people, perfectionists included, store personal benchmarks in their minds. The problem is, doing so insulates them from practical evaluation.

When you write down your standards, you can more easily evaluate whether they're practical. This makes it easier to adjust them accordingly.

For example, let's say you want your windows to be spotless. This goal is consistent with perfectionistic behavior. But is it a *practical* goal? Even if you devote substantial time and effort to make it happen, is it reasonable to do so?

In the right column of your paper, next to each unreasonable benchmark, write a more feasible one. For instance, you might decide that your, *"windows should be relatively free of streaks and spots."* They don't need to be spotless. They just need to be clean.

By lowering your standards, you give yourself permission to act without fear of self-condemnation. As a result, you'll find that you're more inclined to take action. You won't be paralyzed by the hypercritical, perfectionistic voice in your head.

REEVALUATE (AND IF NECESSARY, READJUST) YOUR EXPECTATIONS

~

We need to distinguish between standards and expectations. Standards are the goalposts. In the context of performance, they represent a level of caliber, and imply that any performance that fails to meet or exceed that level is unacceptable.

Expectations embody our convictions that a particular outcome will occur. We believe in the outcome so strongly that we're left befuddled, dispirited, and even angry, when it doesn't happen.

For example, let's suppose you're an Expert level chess player and will be competing in an upcoming tournament. As a perfectionist, you expect yourself to perform flawlessly. Mistakes are unacceptable. This is your self-imposed *standard,* and the one by which you're going to measure your performance.

Let's also suppose that you anticipate winning the tournament. You figure that if you perform flawlessly, there's no reason to presume any other outcome. Winning the tournament is your *expectation.*

The problem with expectations is that their fulfillment depends on a variety of factors, many of which are likely to lie beyond your control or influence. This means there's a good chance you'll be disappointed.

As a perfectionist, you're likely to internalize a negative outcome - i.e. an outcome that fails to meet your expectations - as a personal failure. Can you see the problem with this mindset? You don't hold absolute sway over your circumstances. This being the case, outcomes lie outside your jurisdiction. Yet, you internalize the nonfulfillment of your expectations, as a reflection of your inadequacies.

In other words, investing yourself in false, unjustified expectations is setting yourself up for failure.

In the previous section, we talked about adjusting your unrealistic *standards.* It's just as important to evaluate whether your *expectations* are unrealistic, and adjust them accordingly. After all, the former spring from the latter.

EXERCISE #7

CONSIDER a project you intend to tackle. It could be a work-related assignment, such as giving a presentation to your coworkers. Or maybe it's a home-based activity, such as cooking a new meal. Or perhaps the project is related to a personal undertaking, such as planning a family vacation.

In Exercise #6, we used a sheet of paper divided into two columns. Let's do the same thing here. Grab a clean sheet, and draw a line down the middle.

In the left column, write down your expectations for the upcoming project. Don't hedge for the sake of this exercise. As a perfectionist, it's almost a certainty that you'll have lofty expectations. Write each one down in the left column.

Now, ponder each one. Ask yourself whether the outcome you expect is guaranteed. If not, lower that expectation. Write the adjusted expectation in the right column of your paper.

For example, suppose you're planning a family vacation. You reserve accommodations at a 5-star hotel. Your initial expectation might be that your stay will be perfect. You'd write such in the left column.

But is this assumption realistic? Consider: you have no control over the volume of noise coming from adjacent rooms. You don't control whether obnoxious guests use the pool. Nor do you control the quality of the food at the hotel's restaurants.

In other words, your expectation that your stay will be perfect may be idealistic. Thus, it's worth adjusting your outlook. You'd then write your adjusted expectation in the right column of your paper.

The purpose of this exercise is twofold. First, it's

designed to help you identify unreasonably high expectations that ultimately lead to disappointment, frustration, and self-criticism. Second, it'll help you to grow accustomed to replacing these lofty expectations with level-headed ones.

This reality check is integral to curbing your perfectionistic tendencies.

REMOVE YOURSELF FROM THE
COMPETITION

~

Perfectionists thrive on others' approval. This approval has a substantial influence on their sense of self-worth. As their thinking goes, if others approve of them, they must be worth something.

In many perfectionists, this mindset triggers a crazed level of competitiveness. Everything - every action, every task, and every endeavor - becomes a competition. In cases where the perfectionist is the sole participant, he or she competes against his or her past accomplishments.

This innate competitiveness is more than a mere personality trait. It stems from a need to be perceived as "the best" - the best student, the best manager, the best cook, the best [fill in the blank]. This desire motivates the perfectionist to abandon other pursuits, allowing his or her competitiveness to eclipse other priorities.

This has a deeply harmful effect on the perfectionist. Over time, his or her relationships suffer. His or her stress levels increase. Feelings of inadequacy are reinforced. It can also lead to competitive anxiety, a state commonly observed in athletes.

There's one sure way to curb this behavioral pattern: stop thinking of yourself as a competitor in a contest. Remove yourself from the competition.

This radical change in perspective requires you to do three things. First, decouple your sense of self-worth from others' approval. Recognize that external validation is unnecessary.

Second, acknowledge that there's seldom a need to be "the best" at anything. In most cases, the pursuit of being the absolute best is predicated on seeking external validation. It's a fool's errand.

Third, accept that you can excel at anything without being "the best." In fact, you're likely to experience more growth and develop multiple areas of expertise when you're not hyper focused on dominating one single practice.

Don't compete to be the top contender. That'll only fuel and reinforce your perfectionistic behavior. Instead, identify your values and convictions, strive for excellence, and look for opportunities to expand your personal and professional development.

Your inner critic will have a lesser impact on your emotions when you stop caring about being the best.

EXERCISE #8

THINK about an activity for which you take pride in doing well. No one does it better. Consequently, everyone praises your expertise.

Ask yourself the following four questions:

1. Does my sense of self-worth increase when other people praise my expertise?
2. How would I feel if someone else developed greater mastery over the activity in question?
3. Would I feel successful without being acknowledged as "the best?"
4. What are the benefits of removing myself from the competition?

When you scrutinize an activity through a lens shaped by these four questions, you challenge the assumption that you must be the best at it. As long as you answer each question honestly and reflectively, you'll see that perfectionistic competitiveness is unhealthy and harmful.

REMIND YOURSELF THAT NO ONE IS
PAYING THAT MUCH ATTENTION

~

Perfectionists are their own worst critics. Every minor mistake we make seems significant. Each one makes us wince, giving our inner critics the green light to ridicule our imperfections and perceived deficits.

The result? We torture ourselves over blunders we believe to be catastrophic, when in reality, they're likely to go unnoticed by everyone else.

Other people tend to overlook mistakes that make us, perfectionists, cringe with embarrassment. They're simply not paying that much attention.

Here's an example from my past:

I mentioned earlier that I used to play guitar. I'd record myself on a portable 4-track recorder, and appraise my timing, accuracy, improvisational skill, etc. I'd listen for weak spots.

This process always ended with severe self-criticism. Everything sounded wrong to my ears. If my timing was solid throughout a song, but I missed a couple beats, I'd consider my timing terrible. If my phrasing was clear, but one or two notes were fuzzy or muddled, I'd lambaste my lack of accuracy.

Instead of using this process as a way to improve my playing, I used it to criticize myself.

But here's the interesting part: nearly everyone I played the tapes for - this was before the age of digital recorders - failed to notice my mistakes. The few who *did* notice them considered them to be trivial. The mistakes highlighted areas for improvement, but weren't the disasters I presumed them to be.

In short, few people paid that much attention to them.

You want others to think you're skilled, knowledgeable, and effective. But this doesn't mean you need to be perfect. You can be proficient and imperfect at the same time.

Recall from earlier the importance of giving yourself permission to make mistakes. Mistakes are learning opportunities that'll fuel your personal and professional growth. Additionally, the fact is, most people will overlook them or consider them to be of negligible consequence.

The perfectionist considers each mistake to be a sign of his or her inadequacy. But that self-defeating perception is seldom shared by others.

Most people are just not paying that much attention.

EXERCISE #9

RECALL the last time you made a mistake. Ask yourself how it affected other people's perception of you.

Did the mistake cause others to think you ineffectual? Probably not.

Did they consider you dimwitted? Certainly not.

Did others judge you as unprofessional? No.

You'll probably find that most people failed to notice the mistake. They weren't paying attention. And if they *did* notice it, they probably dismissed it as unimportant.

Each time you make a mistake, put it under the microscope. Examine it rationally, asking yourself how it influenced the manner in which others see you. With time, it'll become clear that the majority of your mistakes are going unnoticed, or are being disregarded as minor.

BE WILLING TO EXPLORE OUTSIDE YOUR COMFORT ZONES

~

The prospect of doing something unfamiliar is extremely vexing to perfectionists. It carries the potential for failure. Perfectionists prefer the safety and predictability associated with their comfort zones.

The problem is, avoiding unfamiliar territory reinforces perfectionistic behavior. Remaining within your comfort zones also encourages your inner critic.

Why?

As a perfectionist, you hold yourself to impossible standards in your areas of expertise, and judge yourself more harshly as a result. When mistakes happen (and they always do), this unreasonable expectation of flawlessness invariably leads to negative self-talk, anxiety, and feelings of guilt and shame.

These negative feelings make you even *less* inclined to explore uncharted waters. After all, if your performance is regrettable in your areas of expertise, how much worse will it be when you try something new?

It's a vicious cycle.

The most effective way to correct this harmful mindset is to face it head on. First, confront your fears of exploring outside your comfort zones. Second, scrutinize them, one by one, to gauge their veracity. Third, decide to challenge yourself.

Venturing into unfamiliar territory is like any habit. It's difficult, even scary, at first. But it becomes easier with time. And each time you do it, the apprehension you feel dwindles bit by bit. Eventually, challenging yourself will become second nature.

Pushing the boundaries on your comfort zones will play a crucial role in curbing your perfectionism. But fair warning: the road to that end is a long one. Here's an exercise that'll help you make the journey.

EXERCISE #10

DIVIDE A PIECE of paper into two columns. In the left column, write down a list of activities you believe are worthwhile, but make you feel awkward or uncomfortable. Here are a few examples:

- Giving a speech
- Hugging a friend you seldom hug
- Asking someone on a date
- Volunteering to oversee a work-related project
- Cooking a new meal with an unfamiliar recipe
- Making a decision in a group of indecisive people
- Writing a letter of thanks to someone you admire

In the right column, write down the worst possible thing that can happen if you do each of these activities.

For example, what's the worst that can happen if you hug a friend you don't normally hug? He or she might look strangely at you, but what does that matter? You're showing sincere affection. Who but the most solemn, humorless curmudgeon could fault you for that?

What's the worst that can happen if you cook a new meal? Sure, you might botch the job. But so what? Every great chef has botched plenty of dishes in his or her career. Each incident is a learning opportunity. Besides, if the new dish is inedible, you can always order takeout.

The purpose of this exercise is to erode your fear of stepping outside your comfort zones. It's to underscore the fact that, while challenging yourself may produce less-than-perfect results, doing so is no cause for stress or anxiety. In fact, stretching your boundaries can be exciting and deeply rewarding.

And importantly, it's a great way to confront and neuter your inner critic.

COMMIT YOURSELF TO AN 80/20 WAY
OF LIFE

~

You may have heard of the Pareto principle. Named after the Italian economist Vilfredo Pareto, it states that 80% of observable outputs are brought about by 20% of observable inputs.

For example, 80% of a salesperson's sales stem from 20% of his or her presentations to clients. Eighty percent of a company's revenues comes from 20% of its customers. Eighty percent of your investment portfolio's capital appreciation is due to 20% of the stocks you own.

You can also apply the Pareto principle (also known as the 80/20 rule) to your daily life. The challenge is, this principle is the antithesis of perfectionism.

Here's an example:

Suppose you're planning to clean your home. Let's also

suppose that doing a "perfect" job will require five hours. The 80/20 rule suggests that one hour (20%) spent cleaning will allow you to accomplish 80% of the job.

The perfectionist instinctively considers this tradeoff to be unacceptable. To him or her, a job that's not done perfectly (i.e. 100%) is not worth doing.

The non-perfectionist, unburdened by inflexible, unreasonably high standards, has a different - and arguably healthier - perspective. He or she isn't interested in doing things perfectly. Instead, the priority is to make optimal use of his or her time.

In our example, this means cleaning for one hour and using the remaining four hours to work on other tasks.

The Pareto principle is highly useful toward overcoming perfectionism. It puts constraints on the time and effort that can be devoted to a particular task. This forces the perfectionist to adopt practical (i.e. lower) standards, and shows him or her that doing so usually produces sufficient results.

Adopting the Pareto principle, and applying it to everything you do, will disarm your perfectionistic impulses. It'll reveal that "good" is good enough, and obsessing over perfection is a dubious use of your time and attention.

EXERCISE #11

DIVIDE A PIECE of paper into two columns. In the left column, write down the things you do on a daily or weekly basis. These are activities for which you take pride in doing flawlessly.

Following are a few examples:

- Washing the dishes
- Exercising at the gym
- Authoring a novel
- Cooking meals
- Responding instantly to texts from friends

In the right column, write down ways to apply the 80/20 rule to each activity.

Let's use exercising at the gym as an example. Suppose you normally perform a carefully-designed workout regimen each week. This routine works your arms, legs, chest, and abdominals on alternating days. It includes strength training, resistance training, and endurance training (also on alternating days).

How might you apply the Pareto principle to this workout regimen?

Note that you don't have to stick to a strict 80/20 model to benefit from this principle. The key is to focus less on "perfect" and more on "plenty."

For example, your "perfect" weekly workout regimen may include 20 different exercises. Suppose you could reduce the number by half and still enjoy most of the benefits. This might be possible if there's redundancy between them.

You might also reduce the number of days you visit the

gym each week. Rather than working out six days a week, reduce the number to five.

You can also replace select isolation exercises with compound exercises that work the same muscle groups. This would effectively reduce the amount of time you spend in the gym while having little impact on your results.

Do this for each of the activities you listed in the left column of your paper. Then, commit to experimenting with each of the 80/20 applications you've brainstormed.

With time, you'll notice that doing things at 100% is not only unnecessary, but also a terrible waste of your time and energy.

MAKE DELIBERATE MISTAKES

~

E arlier, we talked about the importance of giving yourself permission to make mistakes. Here, we're going make them *on purpose*.

Nothing desensitizes perfectionists more effectively than making mistakes, over and over, while performing familiar routines or participating in familiar activities. Each successive mistake makes the previous one seem less consequential.

To be clear, making mistakes is incredibly vexing to perfectionists, especially in the beginning. The first mistake can be absolutely paralyzing because it eliminates any possibility that they'll achieve their primary goal (flawlessness). This is the point at which many perfectionistic individuals give up and return to their comfort zones, feeling defeated.

But if you stick with it, and continue to make mistake after mistake - regardless of how exasperating doing so is - you'll eventually become desensitized to them.

Here's a personal example:

I enjoy playing chess. It's a game in which a single blunder can mean the difference between winning and losing.

Years ago, whenever I made a bad move, I'd be ready to concede defeat. But defeat was neither certain nor imminent. I was inclined to give up out of sheer frustration at myself. My perfectionism would brook no errors.

Over time, I resisted the impulse to give up immediately after my first blunder. I continued to play, and I continued to make mistakes.

I learned something interesting in the process: while each error grated on me, none seemed as consequential as the first one. And the more I made, the less grating they became.

This allowed me to enjoy playing the game while recognizing my performance was less than perfect. I became desensitized to my lack of mastery, and adjusted my expectations accordingly.

There's useful insight in making mistakes. When you're willing to learn from them, they teach patience and increase your resolve. They help you to be more tolerant of your missteps while reinforcing the belief that they're of little consequence over the long run.

EXERCISE #12

THIS EXERCISE IS both simple and flexible. You can do it anywhere. The only requirement is your willingness.

Think about your plans for today. Then, come up with ways to make *deliberate* mistakes.

For example, suppose you're meeting a friend at Starbucks. You usually order a Caffè latte. This time, order a cappuccino.

Suppose you're scheduled to play tennis with a friend this afternoon. Intentionally miss a serve.

Suppose you're writing an email to a coworker. Purposely misspell a word.

This exercise may seem silly. But it has a purpose. It's designed to lessen your fear of making mistakes by desensitizing you to them. It'll show you that few mistakes are momentous enough to agonize over, a hallmark of perfectionistic behavior.

DO SOMETHING AT WHICH YOU'RE UNSKILLED

~

Are you fearful of tackling unfamiliar projects? Does the thought of participating in a new-to-you activity cause you anxiety and discomfort?

If so, you're not alone. Most perfectionists feel the same way. The distress stems from feeling they're not in control. Perfectionists believe their lack of control will lead to failure, which will ultimately reinforce their sense of shame, inadequacy, and low self-worth.

This is the reason perfectionists who hold themselves to impossibly high standards rarely try new things. They don't want to look silly. Nor do they want to reveal their short-comings.

In essence, they don't want to fail.

What's the best way to counter this mindset? Head-on, of course.

As we noted in previous sections, perfectionistic individuals harbor an unhealthy attitude toward failure. They perceive failure as evidence of ineptitude or incompetence. In reality, failure is simply feedback about what works and what doesn't work. It shows us how to improve.

Failures are learning opportunities. Nothing more.

This healthier, positive mindset gives you the freedom to try new things without fear of self-recrimination. Your inner critic knows in advance that you lack experience in the activity you've chosen to pursue. It may try to convince you that you're going to fail. But its voice is impotent because you've already accepted failure as a potential - and importantly, harmless - outcome.

For example, suppose you'd like to learn how to cook. You've never done it before, so there's a high likelihood you'll make mistakes. You know this in advance so you're prepared for it. Plus, you recognize that the worst possible outcome is that you ruin a meal.

Big deal. That's not a catastrophe. Far from it. It's a *learning opportunity*.

Tackling unfamiliar projects and participating in new-to-you activities will make you feel uncomfortable. Your inner critic will sound the alarm, and try to persuade you to desist. But doing something at which you're unskilled while accepting that you might do it poorly is liberating. And it's an effective way to slowly whittle away your perfectionistic tendencies.

EXERCISE #13

WRITE DOWN A LIST of activities you've been reluctant to pursue due to inexperience and fear of failure. Here are a few examples:

- Learning to play a musical instrument
- Giving a speech
- Painting with water colors
- Dancing in public
- Changing the oil in your vehicle
- Writing a short story
- Exercising at a gym
- Joining a book club
- Singing karaoke
- Visiting a gun range
- Volunteering for a charity
- Starting a conversation with a stranger

Next, consider the types of mistakes you might make in the process of doing each one.

For example, suppose you'd like to write a short story. In the process of doing so, you might make spelling and grammatical errors. You may flub the plot structure (setup, conflict, etc.). You might get the voice and tone wrong. Your writing may be dull, or you may include too many impertinent details. Your dialogue might sound unnatural.

Now, stop for a moment. Ask yourself how you might improve or correct each mistake. For example, you can resolve spelling and grammatical errors by hiring a proof-reader. You can resolve issues with your plot structure by hiring a developmental editor. You can tighten and refine your voice and tone by reading books from your favorite authors.

And you'll improve along the way. The process of taking action and seeking *corrective* action when mistakes arise serves as valuable instruction. Moreover, it shows your inner perfectionist that lack of proficiency is no reason to fear doing new things.

REFRAME HOW YOU PERCEIVE CRITICISM

~

I t's difficult to accept criticism with grace and poise. When someone calls attention to a mistake, poor decision, or flaw in our performance, it's natural to feel defensive.

It's not just you. This reaction is universal. Even those who are outwardly gracious when they're criticized are tempted to justify their actions.

Perfectionists have an especially tough time handling criticism. Any critical evaluation of their performance triggers a rash of negative emotions. They become angry, both with themselves and the person offering the critique. They experience paranoia, fearing they'll be revealed as frauds or incompetents. Feelings of discouragement and shame emerge as their inner critics use the criticism as validation of their uselessness.

The reason criticism has such enormous power over perfectionists is because they perceive it as a personal attack. They view it as a declaration that they're neither good enough nor smart enough. They regard it as an assertion of their inevitable failure and lack of worth.

But none of these perceptions is true. When people offer constructive criticism, they do so to be helpful. They notice things we can improve, and provide feedback to that end.

This feedback is invaluable because each of us has personal and professional blind spots, or areas in which we lack awareness. Allowed to persist, these blind spots stunt our development. We need others to assess our performance to help us recognize where and how we need to improve.

This isn't to suggest that all criticism is useful. Nor is all of it intended to be helpful. But that's not important. The salient point is that reframing how you perceive criticism will prevent negative emotions and feelings from overwhelming your rationale. It will also make it easier to deconstruct the untenable claims of your inner critic.

I don't mean to imply that changing your perception of criticism will be easy. It won't be. But the following exercise will help.

EXERCISE #14

THINK of the last time someone offered you constructive criticism. Write down the things this person noted about your performance.

Now, determine the veracity of his or her appraisal. Consider each statement and ask yourself: is it accurate?

Next, ask yourself whether the person offering criticism meant to be helpful or hurtful.

Then, think about how your performance might improve if you were to incorporate the person's advice.

Finally, ponder whether you truly believed your performance was perfect prior to receiving the appraisal.

Here's an example:

Suppose you cook a new meal with an unfamiliar recipe for a friend. Following the meal, you ask your friend for her opinion.

She begins by saying the meal was delicious. She then points out that it could've used a little more salt and seasoning. She also notes that the protein was a bit dry.

First, determine whether her critique is accurate. Accept that she's being truthful even if you disagree with her assessment.

Second, ask yourself whether your friend is trying to be helpful or hurtful. The former is almost certain to be the case. If the latter is true, you can dismiss the appraisal out of hand.

Third, consider how the meal might improve if you were to take your friend's advice and incorporate changes. Would including a bit more salt and seasoning give the meal extra zing? Would ensuring the protein was moister give it a more pleasant texture?

Fourth, honestly appraise your skill level. Did you truly believe you were a flawless chef?

This exercise will help you to regard constructive criticism with a logical, rational outlook. It'll dampen the negative emotions that might otherwise bubble to the surface, and prevent you from feeling defensive and responding in anger. It'll also underscore the fact that criticism is merely feedback. And rather than being a form of condemnation, it's an integral part of your personal development.

COMMIT YOURSELF TO BEING AN OPTIMALIST

~

T he basic credo of perfectionism is that anything that's less than flawless is unacceptable. If a task or project cannot be done perfectly, it shouldn't be done at all.

This mindset causes the perfectionist to focus on failure. Forward progress is ignored as flawlessness is the exclusive goal. Consequently, the perfectionist frets over every detail, many of which are meaningless, toward that end.

This self-defeating habit not only leads to frustration, loss of confidence, and negative self-talk, but also hampers the perfectionist's productivity. Tasks and projects end up taking far more time than necessary. Worse, the time spent on them doesn't produce corresponding dividends.

The time is wasted.

Contrast this mindset to the mindset of an optimalist. An optimalist recognizes that failure is an ever-present possibility. He or she also acknowledges that time spent pursuing flawlessness is time squandered. In that light, the optimalist pursues the course of action that's likeliest to produce the best results with the least amount of time, effort, and other resources.

To be clear, the optimalist is no less interested in success than the perfectionist. The difference is in how he or she *defines* success. It has nothing to do with flawless execution. Nor is it about effecting perfect results. Rather, the optimalist defines success as achieving the best output possible with the least amount of inputs.

In this way, optimalism is a cousin to the Pareto principle (i.e. the 80/20 rule).

So, how do you adopt an optimalist mindset? To be fair, it's a radical change for the lifelong perfectionist. It won't happen overnight. But if you're willing to scrutinize and challenge your current beliefs, you're halfway there. All that's left is to take consistent action toward changing your perspective.

The first step is to acknowledge that making forward progress is more important than perfection.

The second step is to concede that the difference between "success" and "failure" is less clear than you might have assumed. The definitions are anything but absolute; both stem from your mindset.

The third step is to recognize that being flexible and

adaptive to your circumstances is a surer path toward personal achievement than pursuing perfection.

As with any type of habit development, the process of replacing perfectionism with optimalism is a marathon, not a sprint. Following is a simple exercise that'll help you to reach the finish line.

EXERCISE #15

THINK about an activity you take pride in doing perfectly. Then, write down the many ways in which you can adopt an optimalist mindset toward this activity.

For example, suppose you're an author. You're working on your next novel. Normally, you write near-perfect first drafts. The problem is, doing so means you must be meticulous while writing, a process that slows you down and severely limits your output.

Here are a few ways to adopt an optimalist mindset with the goal of increasing your writing productivity:

- Refuse to edit while you write. If you misspell a word, let it go and continue writing. You'll catch the error during the editing phase.
- Don't change your novel's plot structure while you write. If you feel changes are needed, make them during your non-writing time.
- Refrain from researching details while you write. Instead, insert "{XYZ}" as a placeholder,

and keep writing. Research necessary details during your non-writing time.

- Stop worrying about choosing the perfect words. That destroys your creativity. While both story and prose are important, most readers consider the former to be more important than the latter.

I'm not suggesting you cut corners and deliver a less-than-stellar product or performance. Rather, in adopting an optimalist mindset, you're recognizing that perfection is impossible. You're also teaching your brain that the *pursuit* of perfection is a productivity killer.

SET TIME LIMITS FOR TASKS AND PROJECTS

~

I'm an enthusiastic advocate of Parkinson's law. This law states that "work expands so as to fill the time available for its completion."

Productivity-minded individuals regularly use Parkinson's law to accomplish more each day. By limiting the amount of time they spend on any given task, they end up finishing the task in less time than they would otherwise take. Throughout the course of a typical day, this results in a significant productivity boost.

Parkinson's law has another important, yet often-overlooked, application: to help conquer perfectionism.

A perfectionist will work on a task or project until he or she feels it is perfect. The downside of doing so is wasted time. When "good enough" will suffice, perfection is an unnecessary luxury, and oftentimes a costly one.

By imposing a time limit on a task or project, the perfectionist must commit to walking away from it, even if it's imperfect. The time limit eliminates the option to continue making improvements past the point that such improvements make a meaningful difference.

The advantage of doing this is that it prevents your perfectionistic behavior from getting in the way of task completion. Setting time limits keeps your perfectionism in check.

But that's not the end of it. Applying Parkinson's law to everything you do offers an additional benefit. It resets your perception regarding the importance of flawlessness. When you're forced to turn in imperfect work, you quickly learn that doing so seldom carries notable consequences.

In most cases, perfection is unwarranted. Your brain learns that "good" is usually good enough. This new, healthy perspective sweeps the legs out from under your inner critic.

In the following exercise, we'll focus on applying Parkinson's law to activities you normally execute to perfection.

EXERCISE #16

WE'LL START in the same manner we started Exercise #15. Think about an activity you take pride in doing perfectly.

Now, consider how much time it normally takes you to complete this activity. Next, impose a time limit that significantly reduces the amount of time you have available.

For example, suppose you intend to clean your home. You normally need five hours to make it appear spotless. This allows for vacuuming and mopping the floors, cleaning the countertops, washing the dishes, dusting and polishing the furniture, cleaning the appliances, washing the windows, sweeping the patio, and more.

Now, impose a challenging time limit upon yourself. For instance, rather than allowing yourself five hours, give yourself *two* hours. Then, get as much cleaning done as possible in those two hours.

You'll find that limiting your time does three things. First, it forces you to work more efficiently. You're less inclined to waste time because there's less to waste.

Second, it forces you to abandon your perfectionistic proclivities (if only temporarily). You don't have time to worry about trivial details. Consequently, the tiny spot on your living room window no longer matters. Nor does the errant leaf on your patio or the overlooked dust bunny in a corner of your kitchen floor. You don't have time to be perfect.

Third, it gives you the freedom to walk away. No longer do you feel compelled to work until you've met your impossibly high standard of perfection. You've done the best job you possibly can in the allotted time. And that's good enough.

If you apply Parkinson's law to everything you do,

you'll find that your inner critic has less influence over you. Its claims that you're less than perfect will no longer feel as judgmental since imperfection is your expectation.

"GAMIFY" YOUR TO-DO LIST

~

Gamification is the use of games in non-game contexts. For example, if you're having difficulty getting through your to-do list, you can use games to motivate yourself to complete tasks.

Gamification can also be used to exert control over perfectionistic behavior. You can use game mechanics to break the hold that perfectionism has over you.

First, let's clarify the issue.

Perfectionists struggle to finish tasks and projects. But unlike most people, the reason has nothing to do with a lack of motivation. The reason perfectionists so often fail to complete tasks is because they're unable to let them go. They set unrealistic standards for themselves and continue working until they feel they've met them.

Unfortunately, because perfection is impossible, the work never ends. There's always a way to improve things. The perfectionist has difficulty letting go until he or she makes such improvements.

Here's how you can use gamification to counter this habit:

Normally, to-do lists are "gamified" to reduce the tedium of working on mundane tasks. A competitive element is introduced to spur action, and the individual is rewarded upon task completion. In short, gamification make working through to-do lists more enjoyable.

The same principles can be used to dampen your propensity toward perfectionism.

The competitive element in games spurs you to finish tasks, even if you do so imperfectly. You're highly engaged to perform, but your focus is on task completion rather than perfect execution.

Meanwhile, the rewards inherent in games incentivize your effort. The only way to earn the rewards is to finish tasks, further reinforcing that objective.

How does this help you to conquer perfectionism? The more often you're rewarded for completing tasks imperfectly, the less important perfect execution becomes. Your inner critic will try to convince you that your efforts are inadequate. But the rewards you earn for task completion serve as validation of the opposite.

Following is a simple exercise that'll help you to "gamify" any task, project, or activity.

EXERCISE #17

CHOOSE AN ACTIVITY you feel compelled to perform flaw-lessly. Brainstorm ideas for gamifying the tasks associated with the activity. For each task, come up with a competitive challenge and devise a reward.

For example, let's again suppose you're writing a novel. Here are some of the associated tasks:

- Creating an outline of the plot
- Creating the characters
- Writing chapters
- Writing scenes

One way to gamify your writing productivity would be to challenge yourself to write one chapter in 60 minutes. If you succeed in doing so, reward yourself. Watch an episode of your favorite sitcom on Netflix; take a leisurely walk outside; enjoy your favorite candy bar.

You get the idea.

Another example: suppose you're planning to clean your home. Here are some the related tasks (taken from the previous section):

- Vacuuming and mopping the floors
- Cleaning the countertops
- Washing the dishes
- Dusting and polishing the furniture
- Cleaning the appliances

- Washing the windows
- Sweeping the patio

Gamify each task by imposing a time limit and coming up with a reward for satisfying it.

For example, try to clean your kitchen appliances in 20 minutes. If you succeed, reward yourself. Play your favorite video game; call a friend you've been missing; buy a personal development book on Amazon.

This exercise shifts your focus and priority from flawless execution to efficiency. The self-imposed time limits introduce a sense of urgency while the rewards validate task completion. In this way, gamification underscores the folly of getting things perfect and the more desirable goal of getting things *done*.

SEEK INSPIRATION VIA CONNECTIONS
WITH OTHER PEOPLE

∾

I t's easier than ever to connect with people.
Thanks to Facebook and Twitter, our friends,
colleagues, and family members are literally one
mouse click away. Thanks to email, it's possible to enjoy
substantive conversations with people who live halfway
around the world. Thanks to texting, we can reach out to
our friends and loved ones, and expect near-instant
responses.

But despite having access to these tools, have you
noticed that folks are feeling more starved for connection
and engagement than ever before?

As people, we long to connect with others. We're wired
for it. We adjust our lives to ensure these interpersonal
connections are not only possible, but inevitable.

Connecting with others makes us feel encouraged and inspired. It can even pave the way toward self-discovery.

The problem is, no one connects through perfectionism. Perfectionistic behavior keeps others at bay. It intimidates, demoralizes, and frustrates people.

That makes it difficult, if not impossible, to connect with them.

Perfectionists who are able to set aside their rigid standards and relate to others on a personal level will find that doing so leads to inspiration. We're naturally inspired when we hear others doing great things despite their limitations and shortcomings.

It's human nature.

Connections happen through our *imperfection*, not perfection. We're encouraged and inspired when we connect with people who reveal their flaws and faults, and demonstrate how neither are roadblocks to their success.

Connecting with others may seem difficult at first, especially if you're out of practice. The ability is like a muscle, and it might have atrophied from years of nonuse.

But the rewards are worth pursuing. Personal connections do more than merely give you a deeply-satisfying sense of belonging. They'll train your brain that perfectionism is not only unnecessary for success, but an *impediment* to inspired greatness.

EXERCISE #18

MAKE a lunch date with a good friend. Use the time to truly connect with him or her.

Share your personal fears and concerns. Divulge your self-perceived inadequacies, and describe how they paralyze you with indecision and inaction.

Encourage your friend to share similar details.

Then, share your successes with each other. Describe the triumphs you've enjoyed despite your reservations and weaknesses. I guarantee that connecting in this way will inspire you.

Here's an example from my life:

I have a friend with whom I routinely meet for coffee. During these get-togethers, we share our most recent failings and victories with each other. My friend is candid about his imperfections, limitations, and shortcomings. Despite them, he has a beautiful family, a wonderful home, and a thriving business that's the envy of his competitors. And most importantly, he feels content and fulfilled.

Connecting with him always inspires me.

The more you connect with others, the less impact your inner critic will have on your sense of self-worth. Such connections will reinforce that perfectionism, far from being an asset, is in fact a liability.

FINAL THOUGHTS ON THE JOY OF IMPERFECTION

∼

We've come a long way since the first few pages of this book. You now have all the tools you need to curb your perfectionistic behavior and embrace imperfection.

It's important to remember that being imperfect doesn't consign you to a life of mediocrity. Far from it. You can still be extraordinary.

In fact, you're more likely to achieve greatness *as a result of your imperfections* than despite them. Once you acknowledge that maintaining a state of flawlessness is impossible, you give yourself permission to let go of unrealistic standards. This allows you to make continual forward progress in your life. It thus sets the stage for ongoing personal and professional growth.

As a bonus, you'll avoid the disappointment, frustration, shame, and self-recrimination that are par for the course as a perfectionist.

Being perfect is highly overrated. Worse, it's a trap that leads to chronic unhappiness. The moment you decide to overcome your perfectionistic tendencies is the moment you free yourself to enjoy a more rewarding life!

DID YOU ENJOY READING THE JOY OF IMPERFECTION?

~

Thank you for reading *The Joy Of Imperfection*. I realize your time is limited, and I'm grateful that you've chosen to spend some of it with me.

Now, may I ask you a small favor? Would you take a moment and leave a review for *The Joy Of Imperfection* at Amazon? It doesn't have to be long. Just a few words would mean the world to me, and will inspire others to give the book a try.

One last thing before we part ways. I have several books planned over the next twelve months. I'll be releasing each of them at a steep discount.

If you'd like to be notified when these books are released, and take advantage of the discount, be sure to join my mailing list. You'll receive immediate access to my

40-page PDF ebook titled *Catapult Your Productivity! The Top 10 Habits You Must Develop To Get More Things Done.* You can join my list at the following address:

http://artofproductivity.com/free-gift/

I'll also send you my best productivity and time management tips via my email newsletter. You'll receive actionable advice on how to beat procrastination, create morning routines, avoid burnout, develop razor-sharp focus, and more!

If you have questions or would like to share a productivity tip that has made a measurable difference in your life, please feel free to reach out to me at damon@artofproductivity.com. I'd love to hear about it!

All the best,

Damon Zahariades
http://artofproductivity.com

ABOUT THE AUTHOR

Damon Zahariades is a corporate refugee who endured years of unnecessary meetings, drive-by chats with coworkers, and a distraction-laden work environment before striking out on his own. Today, in addition to being the author of a growing catalog of time management and productivity books, he's the showrunner for the productivity blog ArtofProductivity.com.

In his spare time, he shows off his copywriting chops by powering the content marketing campaigns used by today's growing businesses to attract customers.

Damon lives in Southern California with his beautiful, supportive wife and their frisky dog. He's currently staring down the barrel of his 50th birthday.

OTHER BOOKS BY DAMON ZAHARIADES

∼

The Art Of Saying NO: How To Stand Your Ground, Reclaim Your Time And Energy, And Refuse To Be Taken For Granted (Without Feeling Guilty!)

Are you fed up with people taking you for granted? Learn how to set boundaries, stand your ground, and inspire others' respect in the process!

∼

The Procrastination Cure: 21 Proven Tactics For Conquering Your Inner Procrastinator, Mastering Your Time, And Boosting Your Productivity!

Do you struggle with procrastination? Discover how to take quick action, make fast decisions, and finally overcome your inner procrastinator!

∼

Morning Makeover: How To Boost Your Productivity, Explode Your Energy, and Create An Extraordinary Life - One Morning At A Time!

Would you like to start each day on the right foot? Here's how to create quality morning routines that set you up for more daily success!

~

Fast Focus: A Quick-Start Guide To Mastering Your Attention, Ignoring Distractions, And Getting More Done In Less Time!

Are you constantly distracted? Does your mind wander after just a few minutes? Learn how to develop laser-sharp focus!

~

Small Habits Revolution: 10 Steps To Transforming Your Life Through The Power Of Mini Habits!

Got 5 minutes a day? Use this simple, effective plan for creating any new habit you desire!

~

To-Do List Formula: A Stress-Free Guide To Creating To-Do Lists That Work!

Finally! A step-by-step system for creating to-do lists that'll actually help you to get things done!

~

The 30-Day Productivity Plan: Break The 30 Bad Habits That Are Sabotaging Your Time Management - One Day At A Time!

Need a daily action plan to boost your productivity? This 30-day guide is the solution to your time management woes!

~

Digital Detox: Unplug To Reclaim Your Life

Addicted to technology? Here's how to disconnect and enjoy real, meaningful connections that lead to long-term happiness.

~

The Time Chunking Method: A 10-Step Action Plan For Increasing Your Productivity

It's one of the most popular time management strategies used today. Double your productivity with this easy 10-step system.

~

For a complete list, please visit

http://artofproductivity.com/my-books/

85870432R00097

Made in the USA
Lexington, KY
05 April 2018